THE
RUMMAGER'S
HANDBOOK

Finding, Buying, Cleaning, Fixing, Using, AND Selling SECONDHAND TREASURES

R. S. McClurg

P6.90
/
50PP IN A
CUP

THE RUMMAGER'S HANDBOOK

Finding, Buying, Cleaning, Fixing, Using, and Selling SECONDHAND TREASURES

R. S. McClurg

A Storey Publishing Book
Storey Communications, Inc.
Schoolhouse Road
Pownal, Vermont 05261

*The mission of Storey Communications
is to serve our customers by publishing practical
information that encourages personal independence
in harmony with the environment.*

Edited by Deborah Balmuth
Cover design by Carol Jessop, Black Trout Design
Text design by Greg Imhoff
Text production by Andrea Gray
Line drawings on chapter opener pages by Greg Imhoff
Indexed by Northwind Editorial Services

Printed in the United States by R.R. Donnelley
Third Printing, October 1995

Library of Congress Cataloging-in-Publication Data

McClurg, R.S., 1937–
    The rummager's handbook : finding, buying, cleaning, fixing, using, and sell-
ing secondhand treasures / R.S. McClurg.
            p.   cm.
    "A Storey Publishing book."
    Includes index.
    ISBN 0-88266-894-3 (pbk.)
        1.   Secondhand trade.   2.   Rummage sales.   3.   Flea markets.
4. Garage sales.   5. Thrift shops.   I. Title.
    HF5482.M316   1995
    381('.19—dc20
                                                            94-47930
                                                            CIP

CONTENTS

Preface vii

Part One: SELECTING AND BUYING TREASURES 1

Chapter 1: Buying **3**

   Rummaging Is for Everyone!. 3
   Keeping Records. 6
   Finding Garage Sales 10
   Understanding Prices 14
   Dickering and Negotiating Prices. 17
   Paying 20
   Selecting Your Purchases 22
   Wrapping and Sacking 29

Chapter 2: How Much Is It Worth? **31**

   Researching Prices and Values 31
   Dating Treasures 34
   Inspecting for Flaws. 38
   Finding Treasures 39
   Collections 45
   Secondhand Gifts 47

Part Two: CARING FOR AND USING YOUR TREASURES . . 51

Chapter 3: Cleaning and Repairing Treasures **53**

    Supplies and Tools 54

    Cleaning Treasures. 56

    Basic Treasure Repair Advice 62

Chapter 4: Storing Treasures **71**

Chapter 5: Displaying and Using Your Treasures **79**

    Developing Original Decor. 80

    Creating Display Space. 81

    A Few Display Suggestions. 85

    Set the Scene for the Season or Holiday. 93

    Create a Setting for Dolls and Toys 96

Part Three: SELLING YOUR TREASURES 105

Chapter 6: Holding Your Own Garage Sale **107**

    Buying to Sell 108

    Picking a Date and Time 110

    Choosing a Location. 111

    Advertising 112

    Preparing and Displaying Your Merchandise. 119

    Setting Prices. 121

    Wrapping 125

Chapter 7: Other Ways of Selling. **127**

    Selling By Appointment Only 127

    Selling at Flea Markets 131

Appendices. **135**

    A: Where to Look for Secondhand Treasures 137

    B: Book Resource List 139

Index. 143

PREFACE

This book is for anyone who buys, collects, or sells secondhand merchandise at garage sales (also called tag sales, yard sales, barn sales, boot sales, or who knows what else depending on where you live!), flea markets, and thrift stores. It contains tested, helpful hints about finding, buying, cleaning, repairing, storing, using, and selling secondhand treasures. There are useful tidbits of information for *everyone* including the beginning secondhand shopper, the casual, once-in-a-while buyer, the avid rummager

TERMS YOU NEED TO KNOW

Rummagers *are people who shop for secondhand treasures.* *Rummaging* *is the act of searching for treasures in second-hand marketplaces.*

The popular *secondhand marketplaces* *referred to are garage sales, tag sales, yard sales, barn sales, rummage sales, estate sales, moving sales, and boot sales, flea markets, and thrift stores operated by nonprofit charities. Whatever the vernacular name for this type of sale is in your region, the meaning is the same — a place to rummage for bargains on secondhand treasures.*

who devotes several hours each week to this favorite pastime, the selective collector, and the expert seller who is searching for bargains to resell.

The Rummager's Handbook was written to be used. Highlight useful sections. Write in the margins. Add your own notes. Turn back the corners of the pages.

It really is true that one person's "junk" is exactly what someone else wants or needs. Secondhand marketing has mushroomed into a popular, entertaining, productive activity for thousands of people. It has also resulted in the recycling of many objects which would have otherwise been destroyed or discarded. This book can help buyers get the most for their money, assist sellers in increasing their profits, and present new ideas for people who are interested in collecting and recycling.

PART ONE:

Selecting and Buying Treasures

Haply your eye shall light upon some toy
You have desire to purchase.

—William Shakespeare, *Twelfth Night*

That man is the richest whose pleasures are the cheapest.

—Henry David Thoreau

CHAPTER 1

BUYING

Welcome to the wonderful world of rummaging. This fun-filled activity has exploded into a popular pastime. It's the "in" thing to do.

Rummaging is an enjoyable way to save money, a fabulous way to meet people, and an interesting way to recycle. The growing interest in secondhand merchandise combined with the nostalgia craze has saved many valuable treasures from being destroyed.

Secondhand marketplaces and the people who sell and shop in them are fascinating. There are as many reasons for rummaging as there are people who rummage. Each rummager is looking for something special, but almost all rummagers admit they are also searching for neat stuff and great bargains.

RUMMAGING IS FOR EVERYONE!

You are never too young, too old, too rich, or too poor to rummage. True rummagers are rarely embarrassed. They can be found down on their knees, digging in boxes, and crawling under tables in almost any secondhand marketplace.

Rummagers are frequently intense people. They are determined to acquire any treasures which appeal to them. Some rummagers shop daily while others do so only occasionally. There are enthusiastic rummagers who visit their favorite thrift stores six times or more each day.

Rummagers will travel miles to search for secondhand treasures. They drive from town to town to shop at garage sales. And, they take advantage of vacation time. *Example:* Whether from California or Georgia, rummagers will not pass up the opportunity to shop in a secondhand marketplace in Iowa.

Rummaging Is a Social Event

There is usually almost as much conversation taking place at secondhand marketplaces as there is buying and selling. Buyers and sellers share a common interest. Even strangers are friendly.

A kinship exists between regular sellers and their customers. It is a relationship where people are more than just passing acquaintances. Yet, their friendships are usually confined to the circle of secondhand marketplaces.

Many flea market vendors swear that they really don't make very much money in their profession. Yet, they don't retire — another indication that rummaging is as much social as it is business.

A news story of June, 1991 is more evidence of the popular combination of rummaging and socializing: Sixty rural Iowans chartered a bus at the cost of $19.50 per person for a day of garage sales visits in Des Moines.

One flea market vendor made, perhaps, the best evaluation: "People you meet rummaging are different. They aren't snooty or demanding. They are friends for life."

Rummagers Delight in Finding Bargains

There is almost nothing that someone won't buy sooner or later. Some rummagers buy only select items while others will buy anything and everything that strikes their fancy — especially if the price is right, say a dime or a quarter.

Nostalgic, interesting, unique, and attractive treasures are eagerly sought. Some treasures are bought for functional, daily use or to fit into decorating schemes, while others are bought for investments.

RUMMAGING IS EDUCATIONAL

Rummaging provides a great educational experience! It teaches children how to search for bargains and how to get the most for their money. Rummaging expeditions to garage sales, flea markets, and thrift stores sometimes double as history lessons. Many items youngsters have only seen in pictures and museums can be found in secondhand marketplaces.

Rummaging is also an excellent way to entertain children. Young friends are eager to accompany older, experienced rummagers because kids think the oldsters "get all the neat stuff."

Secondhand marketplaces provide a wealth of information — helpful hints, advice, and bits of information on almost everything from recipes to shingling a house, to which doctor is the best in town. Almost anything you want to know can be learned at a garage sale, flea market, or thrift store.

Some rummagers buy only clothing while others buy only treasures. Still others buy both clothing and treasures.

Young mothers appreciate bargain prices on clothing and quality toys which children quickly outgrow. "Fix-It" supplies for scout, school, or 4–H projects can often be found in secondhand marketplaces.

Rummaging stretches teenagers' allowances. Taking the time to search for secondhand clothing enables college students and working teens to coordinate wardrobes of quality name-brand clothing for economical prices.

College students and newlyweds who are setting up housekeeping can find inexpensive furniture and dishes. Secondhand marketplaces are great for homemakers who want to change their decorating accessories. Many of the senior rummagers I know share the sentiment that their lives would have been much easier if there had been garage sales when they were setting up housekeeping and raising their families.

Senior citizens are delighted with secondhand shopping opportunities. Many of them willingly and emphatically declare that they enjoy rummaging because they get more for their money — especially when it comes to buying gifts for their friends. Another advantage is that many people collect items that can no longer be found in retail stores, but do show up in secondhand marketplaces.

Some of the older rummagers are so enthusiastic and have so much fun rummaging, their attitudes are contagious. They make rummaging more fun for those in their company.

KEEPING RECORDS

Before you embark on rummaging expeditions, you may want to think about keeping records of what you see, find, and buy, as well as ideas you get along the way. Even the beginning rummager who has not yet decided how involved he or she is going to become in rummaging should consider recording rummaging activities.

A Journal Is an Asset

Whether you are a rummager who shops solely for pleasure or one who buys for investment and resale, it is worth your while to keep a journal of your rummaging experiences. It can be as simple or elaborate as you like — as long as it is functional for the writer.

Keep notes about such things as interesting conversations, sale conditions, special treasures and why they were purchased, unusual treasure traits or flaws that weren't noticed at purchase time, cleaning methods and repair techniques that did or didn't work, purchase prices, and any pertinent data that will be useful for your future, personal needs. It is also a good idea to include comments such as "I knew this treasure was forty years old because..." or "I had one just like this when I was five years old." Most important of all, include a description of each object, detailed enough so that either you or a stranger could recognize the item at a later date.

Some secondhand treasures already have a monetary value when they are purchased, and they continue to appreciate with age. If someone in your family will one day inherit your treasures, a journal will be helpful in identifying objects and determining values. This is why it is so important to make descriptions thorough enough to enable anyone to identify the treasure mentioned.

Sometimes, you may actually turn to your journal for research, prices, and selling tips — especially if you are planning your own garage sale. A record of purchase prices shows how much an item can be sold for without taking a loss. Remarks about sale conditions you liked or hated work as a guide for a successful sale.

And, never say, "I'll *never* have a garage sale!" Even the rummagers who most emphatically declare they will keep all of their treasures forever usually end up having a garage sale eventually. A journal equips you to be prepared if or when you decide to have a garage sale.

A USEFUL JOURNAL ENTRY MAY INCLUDE:

- *Detailed description of object*
- *Date of purchase*
- *Price paid*
- *Where it was bought*
- *Why it was bought*
- *Interesting conversations about the piece*
- *Flaws when purchased*
- *Cleaning techniques used*
- *Repairs made*
- *Photograph of object*
- *Estimated age*
- *Reasons for thinking object is valuable*
- *Places you've seen similar objects for sale and prices being asked*

Finally, a journal provides personal pleasure. It is fun to read through and be reminded of pleasant rummaging experiences.

Take Notes As You Rummage

It is difficult to remember all of the details on a busy day of rummaging. So, don't rely totally on your memory; take notes. A one- or two-word notation beside an address on a garage sale list is sometimes sufficient. Or, if time is not a matter of concern, more elaborate notes can be made in a small notebook.

An even better way of taking notes is to invest in a small tape recorder that fits into a pocket or purse. Simply record prices paid and any pertinent information about each sale. These handy little tape recorders can usually be bought for under $20.

Later, transcribe your notes by either hand writing, typing, or entering them into a computer. If you don't have time to transcribe,

RECORD KEEPING WITH COLOR-CODED LABELS

One easy way to keep a record of what you paid for a particular item is to develop a color-coding system.

Use gummed garage sale price tags that come in multiple colors and are large enough to cut in half. Assign a price to each color and then mark each treasure with the label representing the appropriate original purchase price.

For instance: One-half yellow circle equals price under 25¢. A full yellow circle equals 25¢. One-half red circle equals price between 25¢ and 50¢. A full red circle equals 50¢. One-half blue circle equals prices between 50¢ and 75¢. A full blue circle equals prices between 75¢ and $1. More exact prices can be indicated by using a symbol mark of your choice on the stickers.

Items costing more than $1 can be marked with pieces of white adhesive tape or address labels. Symbols can be used to indicate prices, such as check marks for dollars and dots for cents, in quarter allotments. Thus, a cost of $1.50 would be represented by one check mark and two dots while a $4 item would be four check marks.

Garage sale labels, tape, and address labels are also great aids for another form of record keeping — dating items. When buying a new treasure, especially a collectible item, from a retail store, write the purchase date on one of the labels and place it in an inconspicuous place on the treasure. With the label in place, you won't be left wondering at a future date exactly when you bought the item.

The same method can be used for secondhand treasures. Even though you might not know the actual age of a treasure, you can glance at the date label and know how long you have had the item.

consider re-recording your notes with more details to be transcribed at a later date. Be patient. It takes a little time to grow accustomed to talking into a tape recorder — and to listening to yourself!

It is important to make fully detailed notes while the facts are fresh in your mind. To save time ask garage sale hosts to leave price tags on your purchases. It's easier than trying to remember the price on every purchase, and it eliminates the rush to note the price before it's forgotten.

Try Other Methods of Record Keeping

Journals are fantastic records for pertinent information about treasures. But, sometimes you want to know at a glance how much something cost.

It is not advisable to leave original price tags or marks on objects long-term because removing or changing them at re-sale time is a time-consuming task. There is also the risk you will miss one of the originals, and the treasure will show two price tags. Such an instance can cause a potential customer to become irritated and result in the loss of a sale, especially since you are probably attempting to sell the item for more than what you paid for it.

Consider using a color code system for noting original purchase prices. Be inventive. Use whatever code is easiest for you.

Photograph Your Treasures

Take an ample number of photographs of individual treasures and decorating displays. Don't neglect before and after pictures of fix-it projects.

Pictures add substance to your journal. They are also good reference materials, and may provide background for researching future rummaging acquisitions and projects.

Photographs offer another advantage for rummagers who change displays frequently: It is easy to lose track of exactly which treasures were used in different displays. It's easy to think, "Gee, we had something really neat in that display at one time, but what was it?" Pictures answer such questions.

FINDING GARAGE SALES

One can never predict exactly where or when a garage sale will be scheduled. They frequently turn up when least expected. To keep up, you really need to check your classifieds daily.

Many towns and cities have Chamber Of Commerce offices that provide free city maps to anyone requesting them. These maps are invaluable for saving time and gas expense in locating sale addresses.

Make a list of all the sales you want to hit on a particular day and plan a route to avoid unnecessary trips repeatedly crisscrossing back and forth over the same area.

When a large number of sales are being held in one week, it is often nice to schedule rummaging expeditions for more than one day of the week. Plan which sales to hit on which days according to the section of town where they occur. Work one section per day to avoid wasting gas on zigzag trips to sale locations.

Watch for "block" sales where all or most of the residents are participating in a neighborhood garage sale. Such sales are fun and competitive. The atmosphere is like a giant outdoor mall filled with secondhand merchandise. It's interesting, and the added bonus is that it's more economical to walk to ten houses on the same block than it is to drive to ten houses on separate blocks.

On busy days of rummaging filled with many sales, it is easy to lose track of where you are. Don't be embarrassed or hesitate to ask the garage sale host where you are. Failing to do so might result in missing a good sale.

Walk and Save Money

Since one of the main objectives of going to garage sales is economic, add to your savings by walking to some sales. Walk to nearby neighborhood sales when you are not intending to purchase large items you can't carry. And, if you find something large, you can always return home to pick up your car.

Watch for addresses where several sales are being held within a two- or three-block radius. Park your vehicle in a central location.

If you buy a sizeable quantity of treasures at one sale, carry them to your car and walk to the next sale.

Have fun! It's true that some passing motorists who are not rummagers might give you strange looks when they see you carrying a huge stuffed bear, a kerosene lantern, a Christmas tree, or some other unusual treasure down the street. Smile and wave. It is *more* likely that a fellow rummager will stop to ask you where the garage sale was where you found such a neat treasure.

And, if it is one of those unlucky days when no fantastic bargains have been found, there's the benefit of at least having had a good walk.

Decorated stand lamp

Guideposts to Good Sales

Streets lined with parked cars and crowds of rummagers coming and going are good guideposts to garage sales.

How much the shoppers are carrying indicates how good the sales are. There are days when you may go to a half dozen or more sales without finding a single treasure. But then, the very next sale may be a bonanza of bargains. Treasure finds are unpredictable.

Talk to your fellow rummagers. They'll give you directions to good sales and warn against wasting time going to bad sales they've found.

Don't judge a book by its cover. Many sales which look high-priced from a distance produce clean, quality, reasonably priced merchandise. On the other hand, don't always avoid locations that look a little tacky or junky. They sometimes yield the best treasures.

Don't assume sales are canceled because of adverse weather. Rain doesn't stop rummagers. Neither does cold weather — especially since so many sellers hosting sales are now using small space heaters in their garages. However, hot weather does prompt rummagers to shop early. Tiny garages with poor circulation and no fans, and steaming concrete parking lots are uncomfortable conditions for both buyers and sellers.

Repeated garage sales are often held at the same location. This doesn't necessarily mean the same sellers are hosting the sales. Because of this fact, rummagers can either be surprised by finding better merchandise than what was at the last sale or disappointed that it wasn't as good.

Multiple participants having a garage sale produce both advantages and disadvantages. There is usually a larger, more varied selection of merchandise to choose from. But, there can be a disturbing difference in prices. Garage sales hosted by members of more than one generation usually offer an interesting assortment of treasures. And don't be apprehensive when youngsters are involved in hosting garage sales. They are frequently more competent than many adults.

Some sellers turn garage sales into small businesses and have more than one sale each year. This is an advantage when the buyers and sellers know each other, and when the sellers continue to provide quality treasures at reasonable prices. It becomes a disadvantage when the sellers assume the sales are guaranteed ways of making money, and they take advantage of regular customers by trying to sell inferior merchandise at inflated prices.

Some avid rummagers are excellent sellers. Look for sales put on by people you've met at other sales.

Old-fashioned church or charity "rummage sales" are usually fantastic! There is almost always a large variety of both unique and useful high-quality treasures with reasonable prices. The sales are located in churches or community buildings which means comfortable shopping at any time of the year.

Garage sales held during the week instead of on the weekend are usually less crowded. And, the sellers aren't as tired and frazzled.

It is sometimes fun and profitable to search for garage sales, flea markets, and secondhand thrift stores in small country towns.

Keep a record of the addresses of really good garage sales. When attending an exceptionally good sale, ask the host or hostess

GARAGE SALE SAFETY

Be careful as you browse. Watch where you are stepping. There can be numerous items to trip over or bump into. Some sellers don't think about conditions that can be hazardous to shoppers.

One hostess had a garage sale in cool weather. Access to the sale site was through a breezeway. An open stairway leading to the basement was located almost directly across from the door entering the garage. A rummager who was leaving the sale stepped aside to allow a fellow rummager coming to the sale to pass — stepping right into the open stairway. If her husband had not noticed the precarious situation and grabbed her arm, she would have fallen down the stairs. At the very least, there should have been a rope stretched across the opening!

Shoppers must also watch out for their children's safety. Supervise your children. Do not allow them to bang into dishes or other breakable treasures. When buying toys for them, always thoroughly examine them first. Example: A charming Granny doll with a yarn body and a plastic head would never have been suitable for a child. Four-inch-long, sharp bobby pins held the doll's hair in place and tiny, wire-rimmed eyeglasses could have been easily swallowed.

if another sale is planned and when it will be. If there is a future sale date, record it with the address for future reference. If a future sale date is not known, make a notation of the address and watch for it to reappear in the classifieds.

Early Bird Shopping

Many rummagers feel it is essential to be among the first customers to arrive at a garage sale. It is true that shopping early can provide more variety, and rummagers have more of a chance of finding what they want.

There are also disadvantages to shopping early. The crowds are larger. It is more difficult to get around in cramped quarters and to reach merchandise. Sellers are more reluctant about bargaining and reducing prices because it is early in the sale.

Shopping later in a sale usually produces the best bargains, if you can find what you want. And, sometimes you can find the perfect treasure. Remember, not everyone is looking for the same things.

Avid rummagers frequently have the opportunity to indulge in "at-home rummaging." This is when friends, relatives, and fellow rummagers drop in with treasures which they know or think you might be interested in buying. The contributors know the rummager's likes, wants, and needs. This is a great way to add to collections and to acquire items you have not been able to find. And, sometimes, the merchandise is even free. *Never discourage at-home rummaging!* It is extremely enjoyable and helpful.

UNDERSTANDING PRICES

Because of the popularity of rummaging, some sellers think rummagers will buy anything at any price. Refusing to do so helps to curb inflated prices on secondhand merchandise. Keep a critical eye out as you evaluate prices, and don't feel pressured to pay more than you think something is worth.

Don't Pay Antique Prices for Garage Sale Treasures

Refuse to pay high prices for dirty, faulty, trashy junk that a seller is promoting as antique or collectible. Many people who have garage sales set their prices according to those they see on similar items at antique fairs and shops.

If you find a treasure you really like, but the price is more than you want to pay, wait. Chances are it will show up in another secondhand marketplace, and the odds are that the price will be lower or negotiable. *Example:* One rummager found a milk glass vase in a size she needed at a thrift store. The price was 75¢. The customer was certain she could find a similar vase for 50¢ and decided to wait. Two weeks later, she found an identical vase for 25¢ at a garage sale.

One thrift store clerk summed it up nicely when a customer was debating about whether or not an item was too expensive to buy. In a matter-of-fact tone, the clerk declared, "Well, if you think it's too high, don't buy it. I don't buy things I think are too expensive."

Garage sales usually offer the lowest prices of secondhand marketplaces, but that isn't always so. There are instances when garage sale prices are higher than new retail prices. An excellent illustration of this statement is baseball cards. Numerous sellers have been seen trying to sell unopened packages of baseball cards for more than what you would pay for the identical pack in a retail store.

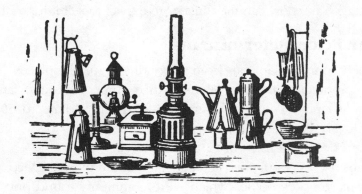

Thus, it is important to know average prices of both new merchandise and of secondhand goods in various marketplaces.

While some garage sale prices are actually high, others just seem inflated. Two dollars might sound like too much for a used, Fisher-Price toy — until you see the same item being sold in a retail toy department for $18. Then, there are times when the same toy can be bought for a dime or a quarter at a garage sale.

Thrift Store Pricing

Two disadvantages of shopping at charity thrift stores are that the prices are usually, but not always, higher than garage sale prices; and, thrift store prices aren't negotiable. However, the higher prices are sometimes balanced out by other factors, such as the time and gasoline expense spent finding garage sales.

Thrift store prices are sometimes frustrating because of their relative variance. One shopper buying a stuffed clown at a thrift store commented that the price of $1.50 seemed a bit high. The clerk agreed, adding that she had just sold a quality jogging suit for the same amount. The relative price inequity is the result of several different people setting merchandise prices.

Watch for garage sale castoffs to show up in thrift stores. It is often easy to identify them because the garage sale price tags have not been removed — which is annoying! If the thrift store price is higher than the garage sale price, don't pay the extra amount unless the item is something you really want. If the item didn't sell for a quarter at a garage sale, how can the thrift store expect to sell it for a dollar?

Other Price Determinants

When items disappear from secondhand marketplaces, they quickly appreciate in value. For instance, three years ago, amber glass relish trays could be found priced from a dime to 50¢ at almost every garage sale. Now, they are found only occasionally, and the price range is from $2 to $10.

Prices rise as people become educated about objects. Decorative Jim Beam whiskey bottles which were commonly found priced at 10¢ to 50¢ several years ago, now have price tags ranging from $2 to $6. The reason is that they have been given a "book value" listed in books about antiques and collectibles.

People who have annual garage sales tend to raise prices with experience. After a couple years of regular, successful sales, many of these sellers raise their prices to the extent that an item that once sold for a nickel is now priced at $1.

The popularity of certain items and their prices varies according to region. One antiques dealer mentioned that she can sell a particular butter churn for $45 in Iowa. The same churn brings $90 in Missouri.

On a more local level, sometimes the location of the sale is a factor in determining the price of merchandise. *Example:* An Avon bottle shaped like a woman's shoe had a $1 price tag at a flea market located beside an antiques mall. The following week, the seller was at a flea market in a small shopping mall and the price on the same bottle was just 25¢.

Comparison shop in your secondhand marketplaces. Check around. Stay tuned to the most current prices for particular items at garage sales, flea markets, thrift stores, and antiques shops.

Sometimes, even the greatest bargain hunter will pay more for an item that will be used as a gift or is needed for a special reason, even though it's not especially appealing. But, the same rummager may deprive *himself* of a special treasure by refusing to pay a higher price. Indulge! Occasional extravagant purchases are balanced out by exceptional bargain prices.

DICKERING AND NEGOTIATING PRICES

For many secondhand shoppers, dickering is half the fun of rummaging. It is a challenge to talk a seller into a reduced, extra-special bargain price.

Some rummagers simply don't think about dickering. Others are too shy to offer lower prices for items which interest them.

Don't hesitate to offer lower prices or dicker back and forth with the seller. Sometimes, dickering doesn't work. More times than not, a deal can be made. At a recent flea market, I offered reduced prices on seven items — six were accepted.

"I'll give you X for this," "Will you take X?," or "What will you take for this?" are some choice ways of approaching sellers.

If you are really interested, don't make your initial offer too low. Give yourself some bargaining space. *Example:* An object is $5. You are willing to pay $3. If you offer $1, the seller might respond that he will accept $4 and refuse to accept anything else. However, if you initially offer $2 and the dealer responds with $4, he or she is more apt to settle for $3.

Many items can be bought for one-quarter of the asking price. Dickering tends to be more successful if you offer one-half the asking price to start out.

Some sellers deliberately place higher prices on merchandise because they expect shoppers to dicker. Other sellers are slow to start bargaining. But, once they realize they're going to sell more, many really get into the act of bargaining. In fact, some sellers become so caught up in dickering that they try to sell you everything they have at reduced prices.

Negotiating Good Deals

Don't be bashful about asking the price of unmarked merchandise. And, remember, you don't have to buy an item simply because you asked how much it costs. If the price is too high, say "No, I don't want it for that amount." The seller might volunteer to reduce the price. If not, make an offer. Failure to ask about price might result in you missing a great bargain. On the other hand, don't be overanxious about learning the prices on unmarked items. Some sellers determine the price by the amount of interest the potential buyer shows.

Being recognized as an avid rummager sometimes offers the advantage of getting good deals. Professional sellers consider such shoppers to be "regular customers." Sellers dicker and make good bargains to sell more and keep the rummager coming back. However, there are times when being recognized puts you at a disadvantage. Some sellers are convinced that avid rummagers are trying to buy things for dirt-cheap prices so that they can be resold.

While dickering is not acceptable at charity thrift stores, don't neglect to call questionable prices to the clerk's attention. Items are sometimes overpriced because an inexperienced person is doing the marking.

Flea market vendors who travel to different regions and set up year-round are less likely to reduce prices. Many seasonal vendors will not reduce prices until the season is coming to an end. But, that is not always true. Some will cut deals all year long to keep regular customers coming back.

Bartering is another option. Perhaps, you have cookie jars you no longer want. There might be a flea market vendor or collector who will trade something you want for a cookie jar.

Some treasures have obvious, but easily repaired, flaws which prompt reduced prices. *Example:* Many small wooden items need only a nail or a little glue to restore them to perfect condition. Yet, a $2 item needing such a simple repair may easily be bought for a quarter or 50¢.

Dickering is Not for All Occasions

Superior quality or extremely unique treasures justify higher prices. Versatility is another reason for paying more for an item. *Example:* A Christmas centerpiece set in a large, wicker basket can be used as is, or the centerpiece and basket can each be used separately. Thus, three treasures are actually being bought for the price of one.

People who are buying merchandise to keep for themselves can afford to pay more than people who are buying items to resell.

Appreciation is the key word! Paying a higher-than-desired price is sometimes justified because the treasure is so thoroughly enjoyed or because it is exceptionally useful.

When a seller refuses to dicker, here are two good reasons for paying the higher price instead of waiting to see if the price will be reduced later in the sale.

1. If the chances are very high that the object will be gone when you go back to buy it.
2. If there is the risk that the object will have been cracked, chipped, or otherwise damaged when you get back to buy it.

Finally, some sellers are so charming that it simply doesn't seem right to ask them if they will take less for their merchandise.

PAYING

When shopping at garage sales, it is an excellent idea to calculate at least the approximate cost of your purchases before paying. Sellers aren't always expert mathematicians. Besides, it is easy for even the most competent person to make a mistake in the hustle and bustle of a large crowd.

One way to help avoid mistakes in calculating the amount due is to discourage sellers from removing prices or sacking merchandise until you are ready to pay for it. When a rummager is finding many treasures to buy, it is common practice to deliver selected items to the location where the seller is collecting money. This frees the shopper to search for more objects without being hindered by those already collected. At the same time, it protects the selected wares from being snatched up by a fellow rummager.

In this type of situation, many sellers try to avoid last-minute calculating and wrapping by keeping a running total of the items and sacking them as they come in. This frequently creates problems. The seller removes the price tags and misplaces them or loses track when helping another shopper. Or, the buyer forgets about an item or two and thinks he is being overcharged. This results in unwrapping, re-adding, and rewrapping — a waste of time and effort for both the buyer and seller.

A tactful way of discouraging the seller from sacking treasures in advance is to simply say something like, "Please don't wrap these things until I'm all through. I might change my mind about something." And ask sellers to leave the price tags on your selections. These simple techniques help avert hassles and aggravation for both buyers and sellers.

Carry Cash

Don't assume sellers, especially those hosting garage sales, will accept checks. Some will, but most are either nervous about accepting checks or flatly refuse to do so. Avoid embarrassing or awkward situations by not asking the seller to take a check unless you have found so many great bargains that you have run short on cash to pay for them all.

It is advisable to carry small bills, fives and ones, as opposed to larger denominations. Many sellers forget they need change. But, even the best-prepared seller can run out of change on a busy day. Also, carry an ample amount of quarters and dimes. Another advantage of using small denominations of money is that there is less margin for error when change is made.

Create a rummaging fund. Throw all of your loose change into a bank or a "change pot." Save it up when rummaging is slow, then cash it in for a special event — perhaps, the best flea market of the year, or an annual weekend that has a reputation for ample sales and fantastic bargains. You'll be amazed how quickly the fund will grow, and how handy it is to have on hand for an exceptional rummaging expedition.

GOOD ADVICE FROM A FLEA MARKET VENDOR

When buying a larger item such as a desk or dresser, you may need to leave the item at the sale location while you go get a vehicle for transporting it. When this happens, take a part of the item with you — such as a drawer — that it can't be sold without. This ensures you that the object will still be there when you return.

The vendor learned this trick after returning to pick up an antique dresser she had already paid for only to have the seller return her money. The dresser had been sold to another rummager who offered more money and had the transportation to take the dresser right away.

Selecting Your Purchases

Once you've found a great sale, the next challenge is deciding what to buy. There are many different reasons for buying.

Rummagers buy treasures because they are fun, functional, or just enjoyable to look at. Some items are bought because of low prices, others because they can't be found elsewhere — unique treasures that you can't go to any old store and buy any day of the week.

Even under the most adverse circumstances, a devout rummager can almost always manage to find a treasure — something he or she simply cannot live without.

Keep a mental or written list of needed items. It sometimes takes a long time to find a specific or unique treasure you are seeking. Be patient. It will turn up eventually! *Example:* In the mid-1970s, long before secondhand marketing soared to today's popularity level, one rummager began searching for a 1963 *Life* magazine containing an article about John F. Kennedy. He finally found the magazine in 1991.

When an object is originally sought casually and not found immediately, the quest for it may become an obsession. Patience will prevail. Then, there are times when rummaging takes uncanny twists in the opposite direction: A rummager wants or needs an object, and finds the treasure the same day or only a couple of days later.

Hair combs

It is fun and sometimes beneficial to go secondhand shopping with a spouse or a friend. Partners can separate and work different areas of the sale location, which is a good idea for two reasons:

1. One rummager might find a treasure which the other has overlooked.

2. If both partners notice the same treasure, it is a *must-buy item!*

Some treasures are bought with no specific use in mind. They just look like something that will come in handy for something, sometime. Another way of putting it is "It looks like something that will be *exactly* what I need someday." This is especially true for people with children.

There are times when rummagers buy a treasure solely because of price — they have no immediate plans for the item, and would have passed it up if the price had been higher. A 75¢ item might not be attractive enough to buy, but an identical item priced at 25¢ might be snatched up without a second thought.

There are also times when there is absolutely no reason or explanation for a treasure's appeal, they just create their own desirability. *Example:* One lady rummager who has an ample supply of candy dish/relish

PITFALLS TO WATCH OUT FOR WHEN SELECTING PURCHASES

- *Buying overpriced items*
- *Buying items that you have no use for, and never will (but they seem too cheap to resist!)*
- *Buying items you don't like (that seem too cheap to resist!)*
- *Buying items without thoroughly examining them first for flaws*

trays swore she was not going to buy any more of them. However, when she found an old, high-quality emerald glass candy dish for a quarter in a thrift store, the thought of how appealing sliced tomatoes or radish roses would look in it was irresistible so she bought it.

Sometimes a treasure originally thought to be "really neat" turns out to be a bad buy because of size, unusefulness, or unnoticed flaws. Then, there are occasions when items bought with skepticism turn out to be valued treasures.

Avoid the Hesitation Factor

The hesitation factor is when a rummager notices a treasure and hesitates about purchasing it because there is a doubt about whether he or she likes the treasure well enough or will actually use it.

When in doubt, *buy!* Under these conditions, unpurchased treasures have a way of haunting a rummager until he or she returns to buy them. Then the object is usually gone.

Part of the rummager's code is, "If you like it, buy it, or someone else is going to beat you to it!" If an item is liked well enough to be considered, it should be bought. Treasures purchased under these conditions usually turn out to be the best-liked and most-used objects.

If you're strongly considering buying an item, carry it around until you make a decision. It can always be returned to a table or shelf if you decide you don't want it. But if it's left to lie while its purchase is being debated, there is a strong probability that it will be lost to a fellow rummager. Never pass up a treasure and then expect it to still be there if you go back to buy it.

There are occasions when an object's potential isn't realized until the rummager thinks about it later. This results in a return trip, wasted gas, and wasted time. One retirement-age rummager sums up the hesitation factor perfectly. She confides, "My husband is always telling me that if I see something I like, I should buy it. But, I'm afraid I won't want it after I get home. Then, I go home, and I wish I had bought it."

Ask Questions

If you are searching for a specific item and you don't see it, ask for it. The seller might decide he has just the thing you're looking for inside and is willing to sell it.

Warning: Many sellers do not research their merchandise. They *think* an item is old, so they put a higher price on it. Such prices are not justified if a seller does not know what an item is or how old it is.

When a seller is asked what an item is, "I don't know" is not a sufficient answer. When asked how old an object is, "I don't know, but it's old" is not a suitable answer. "It was *probably* made *around* 1963" is not an acceptable reply. Anyone can make that sort of statement. Rummagers are entitled to facts, historical information, and documented values.

Pocket compass

When a seller voluntarily announces, "This is old!" ask questions: "Why?" "How do you know it's old?" *Example:* Some fruit jars are quite valuable while others aren't. How does the seller tell the difference? Another excellent example is Christmas ball decorations. A flea market vendor was selling a collection of pink balls for $3 each. The balls were loose in a box, not an original carton. They looked like any round, glass balls that can be bought in today's discount stores. What did the seller know, or think she knew, to justify the price? And shouldn't the seller have been taking better care of the decorations if they were actually worth the asking price?

Every locality has certain brands of products that are extremely popular with rummagers. Home interior decorating accessories are a hot trend in the area where I live. However, there are also rummagers who are totally unfamiliar with local trends. If a seller proudly declares that the item you are examining is "such and such," don't be embarrassed to reply, "That doesn't mean a thing to me. I've never heard of it." A competent seller will inform you about an object. Asking questions is a great way to learn, and it's a good way to do research.

Don't be timid about asking what items are when you don't know. Fellow rummagers and sellers are usually delighted

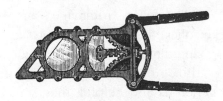

Cattle dehorner

when a rummager doesn't know what something is. It gives them an opportunity to show off their knowledge. Besides, it is much better to ask questions than to wander off muttering to yourself, "I wonder what that was."

Experts come from all age groups and backgrounds; don't hesitate to pick their brains. Youngsters often give the best explanations about what items are and how they are used, and they are great at demonstrating toys. Senior citizens remember when many old items were in use. They can identify objects, explain their purpose, and even help date them.

Asking questions sometimes leads to amusing situations. When one rummager began examining a crystal candy dish, the seller proudly announced, "That's genuine lead crystal from Germany." "How do you know that?" the rummager asked, delighted in thinking the post-retirement-age lady was going to share a secret way of identifying lead crystal. The seller smiled and replied, "There's a sticker on the bottom of the dish."

Get to Know Sellers and Fellow Rummagers

Get to know your thrift store clerks and sellers who set up regularly at flea markets. They can supply valuable information, helpful hints, and fantastic bargains.

Tell flea market vendors and fellow rummagers what items you are looking for. They can be a great help in finding hard-to-locate treasures. Vendors will make a special effort to look for objects and let you know when they find them. They are also extremely cooperative and helpful when for one reason or another you fail to buy a specific piece of their merchandise, but later decide you can't live without it. If you call a seller and ask if they still have the item, most will either save it or get it to you.

Most fellow rummagers are friendly and helpful. Some offer unsolicited advice and information. They are frequently helpful in giving directions to good garage sales.

But, rummagers can be contradictory. While they are *usually* generous and helpful, they sometimes become selfish and vindictive. Some may be afraid you are going to beat them to something they want. Rummagers can be rude and cutthroat, and take advantage of any and every opportunity to be the first ones to reach the treasures. Some avid rummagers have actually been known to grab items they wanted right out of the hands of fellow rummagers!

Using courtesy and good manners is not always to your best advantage with such people. The person you hold a door open for, or allow to go in front of you, might turn out to be a savage, pokey rummager blocking your way. *Example:* One rummager was shopping for wares in a thrift store when another pushing a cart full of clothing approached. The first stepped aside to allow the one with the cart to pass. In turn, the woman with the cart blocked the aisle and began rummaging right in the spot of the rummager who had shown courtesy.

There was even one report of a rummager who was so intense in her shopping that she slugged a woman twice her age in the eye! So, beware the cutthroat rummagers — and welcome conversation with the helpful ones.

Rummaging for New Treasures

Searching for treasures on sale in retail stores is still rummaging. The only difference is that you're buying new instead of used merchandise.

This type of rummaging requires patience to wait for sales, boldness to take the chance that wanted items

---

BECOME A SCAVENGER

Eventually, the most devoted rummagers become scavengers — people who can find a potential use for almost anything.

Scavengers are:

- *Creative*
- *Adept at combining unusual items, textures, and colors*
- *Experienced in combining secondhand treasures with new items*

If you:

- *Begin buying new items on sale that people have passed by because they didn't see a use for them*
- *Begin buying new items on sale specifically to be resold for higher prices at garage sales*

Then, *you have achieved scavenger status!*

won't already be sold out by the time they go on sale, and a knowledge of the store's procedures and of its timetable for after-season sales. Clearance and going-out-of-business sales sometimes offer even better bargains than secondhand marketplaces for new merchandise with cheap prices.

Selective Buying

There comes a time when even the most devout rummagers realize they have to become more conservative. They *have* to stop buying everything they can lay their hands on just because the price is right. Time, experience, overbuying, and, especially, running out of space, prompts a rummager to ask, "What will I do with it?" and "Where will I store it?"

Other contributing factors that lead to selective buying are the realization that too many treasures are not being used to their full extent, that they are nonfunctional, or that they are taking up too much storage space to warrant purchase.

Now, the selective rummager decides to limit purchases to gifts, additions to collections, unique items, extremely high-quality treasures with bargain prices, and objects that are graceful, special, or functional. Sometimes, the selective rummager also begins purchasing items to be resold for profit.

Being selective does not always save money. The rummager buys fewer items, so there is less to use and to store. But, now the rummager tends to pay more for treasures that he or she really likes or wants instead of waiting for bargain prices.

Another disadvantage of being selective is that it may lead to regrets. Before, the rummager bought items on the chance they might be needed for something sometime. Now, the same type of objects are passed up, and the selective rummager is frequently heard to say later on, "I should have bought that!"

Be realistic. Know your priorities. Avoid items that require storage space you don't have and you can't create. Stop buying specific items when you realize they aren't being fully utilized. *Example:* Coke and beer glasses make interesting and attractive collections. Many times they can still be found for 25¢ each at garage sales; antique dealers are pricing them for $4 and up. But, if you aren't using the glasses, you aren't gaining any benefit from them, and they're just taking up a lot of space!

Wrapping and Sacking

Rummagers have the right to expect sellers to supply bags or boxes for carrying treasures easily, and newspapers or other wrapping materials for delicate treasures. However, sellers are not always that considerate or organized.

Be prepared. Take your own sacks with you! Plastic grocery bags fold and fit easily into pockets or purses. But use these grocery bags with caution. At one time they were durable sacks used to transport "tons of stuff" for what seemed like forever; the new, recycled version of the plastic grocery bag tears easily. It is a good idea to double-bag treasures, especially if walking any distance. It would be a shame to lose a really neat treasure because of a torn bag.

Sturdy, plastic shopping bags, canvas totes, and racquetball bags fold nicely, are easily carried under the arm until needed, and accommodate large quantities of treasures. These sturdy bags are safe and durable, and especially nice for block sales and flea markets.

COME PREPARED

You never know what kind of wrapping a seller may (or may not) have on hand. So carry your own wrapping supplies in your car, or purse or pocket. These include:

- Old newspaper or rags for padding (old pillowcases work well!)
- A brown box or two
- Plastic shopping bags that fold easily into your purse or pocket
- A sturdy string bag
- A canvas tote bag with many pockets
- A nylon gym bag that folds compactly

Many of the canvas tote bags have small pockets which are convenient for safely transporting tiny breakables. Nylon gym bags can also be folded into small sizes and are durable enough to carry many treasures.

Some sellers have the attitude that plastic, metal, or wooden objects do not need to be wrapped. But, they do need just as much care as glass and pottery. Plastic *does* break. And, metal and wooden items can be chipped or scratched if they rub against each other.

You paid for your treasures. You have the right to have them protected. Don't allow the sellers to be negligent.

Remember: It is a buyer's market. Don't be intimidated! Ask questions, make requests for sacks, and refuse to buy overpriced or inferior merchandise. Most of the treasures rummagers buy are things they don't have to have — things that can be passed up if the seller doesn't respond to your requests.

CHAPTER 2

HOW MUCH IS IT WORTH?

One of the greatest joys — and challenges — of rummaging is finding treasures that are worth much more than what you paid for them. The value may be clearly established, such as when an item has a book value, or it may be more subjective, such as a piece that matches one of your collections or is particularly useful to you. A treasure's worth is often relative to the rummager's interests and tastes. Some buy items because they just like them or have a specific use in mind — or because they think an item has a higher monetary value than what they're paying for it. The more knowledgeable you are when you're perusing the goods at various sales, the more likely you are to find and obtain objects of worth.

RESEARCHING PRICES AND VALUES

Knowing brands is critical to finding bargains and keeping from getting ripped off. This is especially true of such things as pottery, dishes, fine glassware, or almost any collectible item.

Beginning rummagers encounter dozens of company and brand names they have never heard of before. As time passes, the unknown becomes familiar. Experience prompts rummagers to listen for new names and to learn about them. Even the most expert rummagers have instances when they admit, "I've never heard of that. Tell me about it."

But you can't rely on others to tell you information you want or need to know. Take advantage of the variety of books on antiques and collectibles available at your local library to research all sorts of things. Looking through such books is both fun and educational.

Browsing in antiques stores is another way of researching treasures. But, remember, just because the sign on the door says "antiques," it doesn't guarantee the items are old. "Collectibles" are getting younger every day. And remember as well that the shopkeeper does not know everything. In fact, there are instances when you might be more informed than the person running the shop.

Sometimes, the best way to learn is by just listening to or talking with dealers and fellow rummagers. Rummaging is a constant learning process; there is always something new to learn.

A knowledge of treasures and their values can impress many sellers and persuade them to reduce prices. For example, a seller who is trying to convince a buyer by saying something like, "That's Avon, it's collectible," is apt to reduce the price if he or she discovers that the rummager knows more than that about the product. It is especially persuasive if the rummager can accurately point out that the item is actually worth a specific, lower price.

There is probably not a rummager alive — including the collector with no intention of reselling any owned treasures — who isn't thrilled by finding a 25¢ bargain and learning it is worth dollars more. But, a rummager must know the merchandise in order to make such evaluations. Research is important to *all* rummagers!

Evaluating Pricing Standards

Remember that professional sellers are using many of the same price-guide reference books you are. This can be a disadvantage when they set prices according to the guidebook listings. Because, while most of the books have excellent basic price listings, many do not specify regional values. An item that is worth a certain amount where you live might be worth either nothing or three times that amount in another state. Thus, treasures may gain a reputation as valuable or collectible, even though that might not be the case in your locale. Many inexperienced rummagers think they should always be able to charge book prices for their merchandise. Sometimes they can, but it's usually not the case. An excellent illustration is

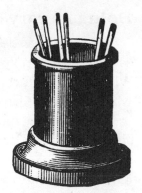

Matchstick holder

Avon bottles. Some of them are worth quite large amounts while others aren't worth anything. Yet, it is not unusual to hear a seller proudly announce, "That's Avon, so it's worth a lot."

Some items are merely status symbols with a reputation for being valuable secondhand treasures. Many sellers believe that because items were expensive when purchased new, this justifies higher secondhand prices. And some think rummagers will be impressed to find expensive items on sale at their garage sale.

Looking through antiques books, you can see how easily a rummager can misidentify an item. For instance, some containers used for holding stick matches are very similar to toothpick holders. Ceramic pin cushions shaped like owls, elephants, cowboy boots, and other things can also easily be mistaken for toothpick holders when the cushions are missing. One item that looked like a candle holder for a pillar candle turned out to actually be a holder for an ink bottle.

I've heard reports of several rummagers who paid 50¢ for what looked like ordinary planters with nothing really significant about them — but their actual value ranged from $25 to $50. These rummagers found the bargains because they knew what to look for; their research paid off.

Novelty pin cushions

Doing Library Research

The reference department in your public library is a valuable asset. It can supply almost any information you want or need: Whether or not a company is still in business, company addresses, which companies have consolidated, and dates of production periods.

Sometimes, a rummager's curiosity is roused about treasures already purchased. If you can't find information about an item in the guide books, and no one else seems to know anything about it, research the treasure yourself. If all you have is the name of the company printed on the treasure or a label, begin there. So long as the company has not gone out of business, its address can most likely be obtained at the library. If the company is not listed, a librarian may frequently be able to tell you whether it is totally out of business or has merged with another company. Sometimes, you may need to begin your search with alternative company names and addresses. Write the company with a detailed but brief description of what you have. Tell them what you want to know. Enclose pictures of your treasure. You might also write a company at times when you need help locating an item you have not yet been able to find. Some companies are extremely cooperative and helpful; others don't respond.

DATING TREASURES

It is sometimes difficult to determine which objects are old collectibles and which are new reproductions. Thus, dating is important. And it is not always easy to do. The obvious, easiest, and most accurate method is buying treasures with dates printed on them. Many new collectibles are dated; some older treasures have dates printed in Roman numerals.

One clue to dating such things as figurines, planters, and pottery is to find out when companies began using labels instead of engraving or printing their names on the bottoms of products.

With time and experience, rummagers can become quite competent at dating some things — especially those types of treasures that interest them most. They learn little tricks for recognizing and dating treasures by listening to conversations of buyers and sellers, asking questions, and developing their own methods.

One of the most interesting ways to date items is through old magazines. Browse through some of the general interest magazines looking for pictures of items you have. The time period of the accompanying article or the date on the magazine cover supplies the era the item was used.

Magazine advertisements are also extremely helpful. Sometimes they help you identify an item you've seen but

Lace bonnet

didn't know what it was. Ads often offer interesting descriptions of the item, its use, where it was made, and how much it cost at the time.

Look for Clues in the Packaging

Zip codes appearing on items may help date the approximate era. According to the library, the zip code came into being in 1963. It was not widely used at that time. Before then, states had three- or four-letter name abbreviations. For example, Wisconsin was *Wis.* and Minnesota was *Minn.* States with short names, such as Iowa, were written out. With the zip code came the two-letter state name abbreviations — *W.I., M.N., I.A.* The one question my librarian could not answer was when the periods were dropped from the abbreviations. But from this information it is safe to assume that a treasure with an address on it containing a zip code was produced after 1963. Those with addresses without zip codes were probably produced before 1963. This most certainly is not precise dating, but it does supply a general era for objects that are hard to identify or date.

UPC bars and the unit of measurement (pounds and ounces or metric) are also age indicators. As with zip codes, UPC bars and

Cocoa packaging

metric measurements were gradually phased into accepted, everyday use. Their presence or absence indicates the approximate instead of exact era. According to information I obtained at the library, the UPC price system originated in the grocery field in 1973. Many older items are labeled with both price bars and actual price tags. The newer the item, the less likely it is to have a price tag.

Data on the origin of metric package labeling is more scant. It has apparently been used in foreign trade and on alcoholic beverages for several decades. According to my research, metric measurements weren't required on familiar, everyday items until the late 1980s. A resourceful librarian leafed through old magazines, using ads to spot-check labeling on household items. To obtain information for a specific product, it would be best to write the company that produced it and ask when its metric system was put into use. *Example:* To research a Brach's candy tin, "32 OZ. (2 LBS.) NET WT.," with a picture of roses on the lid, you could send a picture of the tin, along with a brief description, a notation of any additional writing on it, and the dimensions. From this information, the company may be able to determine exactly when the tin was made.

The age of Coke glass bottles can sometimes be determined by capacity. Twelve-ounce cans or sixteen-ounce bottles were not produced in 1940.

State abbreviations, zip codes, UPC bars, and units of measurement are only a few of the tidbits of valuable information which original packages tell about their contents. But, you cannot always be sure that original boxes contain original items. *Example:* How many people put Christmas tree ornaments back into original boxes, if there are many ornaments to put away? It is possible to find some older ornaments in original boxes when owners didn't have so many to put away or because they grew tired of old ornaments and stored them when they purchased new ones. Don't pay premium prices for original packaging. Pay only what the item is worth to you — not what it might be worth if it is old.

An antiques dealer advised me that one way to recognize aged Christmas decorations is their shape — many are not round balls like the more recent ones. Old decorations usually came in packages of six or twelve, whereas newer ones are commonly packaged in lots of four or five. If your passion is old Christmas ornaments, a good rule of thumb is to be certain that at least one of the ornaments you're buying is worth the price of the entire package.

It is easy to think of plastics as being new, but many of them have been around for decades. Don't dismiss their value.

In dating doll clothes, check the fastenings: Old ones have button or snap closures, while many new ones have Velcro.

A careful eye to appearances is key to dating items. An old, quality, amber candy dish and a replica of it may appear to be identical. On closer look, the old dish has an obvious, satin smooth finish and a gleaming appearance which is missing from the replica.

HIDDEN TREASURES IN OLD PICTURES

Fragile brown paper dust covers on the backs of pictures indicate the pictures are old. In June 1991, a rummager purchased a picture for $4 at a flea market on the East Coast. He wanted to use the frame for something else. When he removed the picture from it, he found one of twenty-four remaining original copies of The Declaration Of Independence. It was sold at an auction for $2.4 million.

Since the news story broke, almost every old picture found in local secondhand marketplaces has had the backing sliced, torn, or removed. Do not randomly slice or tear the backing on old pictures. You don't know what you might be destroying! And, such action detracts from the authenticity and value of the treasure. Remove with care! Treat the backing as if it is also a treasure.

Inspecting for Flaws

The condition of an item affects its value — both monetary and practical. Remember to always inspect treasures closely before purchasing them. It is easy to neglect doing so when you get excited by a neat treasure. The better the bargain, the greater the temptation not to examine it closely. Remember, even a nickel item loses its appeal and value if it cannot be used or repaired. It then becomes junk taking up valuable space.

Don't assume items for sale in thrift stores are perfect. Faulty items sometimes get put out for sale. Some objects are chipped or cracked by careless shoppers. Not all flaws are visible; some are hidden by dirt. Many flaws are found by touching.

When considering an item such as a sewing machine needing "minor" repairs, check with your local service center before buying. Find out if the parts are available and how much they cost. A $20 sewing machine that needs $50 in repairs is *not* a bargain, especially without a guarantee. A typewriter is useless if the ribbon has been discontinued. Beware of computers: Many are obsolete.

I know one rummager who suspects sellers are trying to conceal flaws when price tags are placed over the holes in the bottoms of shakers. Unfortunately, some sellers do deliberately try to sell damaged merchandise. *Example:* An eighty-year-old woman set up at a flea market. She was insulted when a rummager offered a lower amount than

Buying Secondhand Appliances

Don't be shy about testing electrical appliances. Plug them in, turn them on, and test them. You've wasted your money if you buy something and then find out it doesn't work.

A good rule of thumb is decide how much you are willing to lose on an appliance that might not work. Keep the amount low and stick to it. Most sellers are honest about faulty items. Some simply don't know when there is something wrong because the objects don't belong to them.

what she was asking for a pheasant-shaped flower planter. "No!" she asserted, "It's collectible even though it is chipped!" Not so. The chip reduces the value significantly, especially in this case where the entire tip of the tail was broken off.

FINDING TREASURES

"If it seems too good to be true, it probably is" does not apply to rummaging. But, some treasures are such fantastic bargains that they really do seem too good to be true. Even the most experienced rummagers are sometimes surprised by the quantities of new, never-used items that can be found in secondhand marketplaces.

Finding quality items makes rummaging really fun. The treasures grow even more attractive when they are coupled with bargain prices. Sometimes, shopping for new merchandise is dull compared to rummaging.

A sentiment commonly shared by both buyers and sellers is that eventually everything will turn up in a secondhand marketplace. Two of perhaps the most unusual items I've found are a hospital bed pan and a five-foot-tall suit of armor!

There are times when rummagers arrive at a sale late in the day only to find items such as dolls, dishes, toys, or any one of a number of objects that they believe are collectible or have a book value. Yet, because

Suit of armor

it's near the end of the sale, the rummagers are skeptical, thinking "Well, it must not be worth as much as I thought, or some dealer would have snatched it up by now." That's not necessarily true. Don't doubt your judgment or knowledge if you have a good record. Perhaps the seller did not put the item out until later in the sale.

Most dealers want to be the first ones at garage sales, and many of them don't bother with sales in the later stages. Antiques dealers and collectors might not have been to that particular sale, or

Buying Christmas Decorations in Secondhand Marketplaces

Artificial Christmas trees are good buys at garage sales and they're more likely to be complete than those found at thrift stores. Most garage sale sellers will tell you if parts are missing or there are any flaws. Tree parts are sometimes lost in transport or storage, and thrift store sales clerks aren't privy to that information, unless the tree has been assembled. Quality tinsel garlands are scarce. The ones found are usually dirty, tangled, and tattered, and not worth the investment. Quality evergreen garlands and large red plastic bows are also rare finds.

Consider buying strings of Christmas tree lights if the price is cheap enough. Most strings of secondhand lights have plugs on both ends so they can be connected, while many of the newer lights available in retail stores have plugs on only one end.

Secondhand strings of lights sometimes have many missing bulbs, so the seller disposed of them and purchased new ones. Or all the bulbs may be present, but the cord faulty. You can buy strings for a quarter or 50¢, and interchange light bulbs. Check light strings carefully before using: look for breaks in the wires; watch for faulty plugs. Some decorative, seasonal lights — figures of Santa Claus, jack-o-lanterns, snowmen — use a cord with a single socket that holds a Christmas-tree-size light bulb. Most of these cords snap out easily and make an excellent tool for quickly testing individual bulbs. Remember to use caution: Plug the cord into a power strip, wear gloves to protect your hands, and wear safety glasses.

they might not have wanted to pay the price asked for the object. It might not have been seen as a good investment for resale. *Example:* One post-retirement-age gentleman hosting a garage sale had a set of snack plates with matching cups, a style popular in the 1940s and 1950s. The dishes were quality crystal, old enough to be antique, and in excellent condition. The price of the set was only

75¢. People don't use this type of dishes anymore, and antiques dealers in the area of the sale can't sell them so they won't buy them, but that doesn't mean the dishes aren't worth collecting.

Buy It When You Find It

Rummagers search for treasures all year long, frequently planning their collection projects a year in advance. It is necessary to do so because if they decide they need a specific item, they might not find it in a day or so. It sometimes takes weeks or even months for a rummager to find what is needed.

Some treasures are bought *only* for possible future use. Many items are bought because they might not be available when needed. Flower pots are a good example. Decorating accessories and gifts are another.

Friends or relatives who are not rummagers might be shocked or think you're nuts buying Christmas decorations or Christmas trees in March. But sometimes that is the best time to find them. Rummagers buy when treasures are available. Besides, shopping year-round for Christmas decorations and gifts enhances the Christmas spirit.

Watch for "grab bags" and bargain boxes in secondhand marketplaces. Many of them contain from five to twenty-five items and can be bought for prices ranging from a quarter to a dollar. This is rather amazing since almost any individual item in the bag or box could be sold for at least a nickel. So the price of each item averages only pennies.

Sometimes, only one item in a bargain box may draw your attention; the rest may look like trash. But, rummagers are frequently surprised to find many useful treasures in a box. Whenever someone comments, "It looks like a box of junk. What are you going to find there?" you'll usually discover the box contains something you can't live without.

Cracker Jack surprises are fun! Finding treasures is like finding the prize in a box of Cracker Jack: And, it always seems extra special because it's a bargain you didn't know was there. Grab bag purchases almost always have at least one special treasure — something really neat or actually valuable — concealed within.

SOME TREASURES TO WATCH FOR

Old magazines have fascinating artwork and advertisements that may supply pertinent information for dating old treasures. They also contain interesting historical articles that may evoke the memories of senior citizens and rouse the curiosity of youngsters.

Examine old magazines closely before buying. If small articles or recipes have been cut out, the value is decreased.

Entire wall groupings or accessory displays may be available when a seller is changing their decorating scheme. Often such treasures were bought to coordinate with each other and, if they are in perfect condition, make a valuable collection.

Genuine Raggedy Ann and Andy dolls have a trademark of the words "I Love You" in a red heart printed on their bodies. Many other quality dolls have the names and dates printed on their heads, just above the neck or in the buttock area.

Red glass is worth looking for. Sometimes it's difficult to tell when it's real and when it's been painted: Hold the treasure up and look through it from the inside out to detect small scratches or peeling paint.

You may also find other colors of painted glass. Painted glass is not always bad; sometimes it's very pretty and frequently you'll find old, quality, clear glass when you remove the paint.

Cut-glass treasures should be examined closely. Some patterns are more delicate than others. Some catch light better and sparkle more. Some have a more velvety feel.

Miniatures with fascinating, intricate details are worth searching for.

Toys are good buys. Even rummagers who don't have children should pick up at least a few inexpensive, quality toys to have on hand when small people come to visit.

Costumes are often found in secondhand marketplaces, especially children's manufactured Halloween costumes. These are also great places to find clothing and supplies for your own costume creations. Halloween masks are more scarce, but they are usually in good condition if found. Often you can find pumpkins, gourds, and Indian corn for autumn decorating for nominal prices at flea markets as well.

Seasonal produce sold at flea markets is usually high quality, and very reasonably priced.

Bike and automotive parts are good buys at garage sales and flea markets — such as tools, bikes, automobile tires, hubcaps, and seat covers.

Don't hesitate to buy a single piece of a set — a salt shaker, cream pitcher, or sugar bowl. It is more common than not that the companion piece will turn up eventually. It is rumored that some collectors and professional sellers even buy only tops or bottoms of "hens on nests" when the rest of the dish is broken.

If you have just one piece of a salt or pepper shaker and you're looking for a top or bottom to match, take it with you to sales so you can try the lid on the shaker (or visa versa) before buying.

When buying a hurricane or kerosene lamp, don't worry if the glass shade is missing. It won't be difficult to pick one up at a later date.

Clear glass, star-shaped candle holders can be found now and then, priced from 5¢ to $2. Buy this style when you find it at the right price. The stars are attractive and fit well in small places. They are safe because they catch wax drippings well, and they don't tip easily. And some of the older ones are probably collectible.

Small plastic pails are usually excellent secondhand bargains. The price is commonly only a fraction of the item's price when new.

Look for interesting color and texture combinations by pairing treasures you find for sale. Often they can be pleasantly surprising. *Example:* A sleek blue water pitcher matched with cut-glass drinking glasses make a striking, impressive combination.

Watch for good, heavy, sturdy wire hangers, which can usually be found for a penny each. It's always good to have extra hangers on hand and, sometimes, plastic-coated hangers just won't work.

Yarn can often be found in various colors and sizes at bargain prices. *Example:* Just the other day, I bought a box containing thirty skeins of rug yard and two skeins of knitting worsted for $1. None of the skeins had even been opened. Consider buying a box of bargain yarn to have on hand for friends who knit or crochet while they are recovering from an illness.

Replacement casserole lids or dish bottoms can be found in secondhand marketplaces. If you buy a replacement lid that turns out not to fit, don't despair. The style without a knob can be used as a substitute platter, and those with knobs can be saved for use on another dish.

Buy expandable wooden hat peg racks when you see them, especially the style that stretches out to various widths, creating an open diamond-shaped background. The racks have ten pegs, and are commonly used for holding caps, light clothing, or mugs. They are valuable accessories for decorating

and for storing treasures. This is one of the most hit-and-miss treasures to find. There are times when you'll find them at almost every sale, then a long period of time may elapse before you find anymore.

Figurines are scarce. When found, they are usually expensive. Watch for substitutes — character candles, salt and pepper shakers, decorative bottles.

Candle rings are excellent bargains because they are nominally priced and extremely versatile.

Old toys to show up in thrift stores a few weeks before and a few weeks after Christmas. People are getting rid of them to make room for new toys.

Secondhand marketplaces are good sources of collectible toys such as Batman, Mickey Mouse, California Raisins, Smurfs, and Alf. Many parents invest in popular trends and then dispose of the toys when children grow tired of them. *Example:* An Alf doll which sold for around $30 when new was bought for 75¢ in a thrift store.

Every household should have a Cabbage Patch doll. It is amazing how many female visitors comment. "Oh, *you* have a Cabbage Patch doll! I've always wanted one!" Keep the dolls in mind as gift ideas.

Record albums are alleged to be highly collectible because they can no longer be bought in record stores — only through TV promotions. Quantities of records are disappearing from secondhand marketplaces, but I'm not sure who is buying them. Antiques dealers don't seem interested.

Promotional items such as small toys, glasses, cups, and other pieces from fast food places such as McDonald's, Burger King, and Pizza Hut are frequently found at garage sales. Some of these become collectible almost immediately.

You never know where you are going to find a treasure.

Example: I know a rummager who bought a pair of picture frames at a thrift store with copies of Norman Rockwell prints set in them, it looked like a youngster's Cub Scout project. When one of the pictures fell off the wall, the frame came apart and revealed the writing on the back of the print, "State Farm Insurance 1986 Calendar." This would be a real find for anyone collecting calendars or calendar pictures.

"Cheap costume jewelry" of yesterday might actually be quite valuable today. Remember, it wasn't so many years ago when both quality and costume jewelry were reasonably priced. As frequently happens, these treasures might be worth more today than when they were new. Even handmade objects can become collectible because of the materials or molds used in their making.

COLLECTIONS

One beginning rummager asked, "Do two items make the beginning of a collection and mean I am collecting?" A very experienced fellow rummager responded, "When I have three of a type, I usually say that it is turning into a collection."

Toothpick holders

One rummager's knack for noticing — and tendency for buying — toothpick holders created a collection before the buyer even realized it. Many collections begin this way.

Then, there are collections that are consciously decided upon: "I am going to collect figurines of blue jays because they are unusual. Besides, cardinals are too hard to find and they are usually too expensive anyway."

WHO'S BUILDING A COLLECTION?

Starting a collection may be a conscious decision, or it may happen by chance. Two ways it can happen are:

- *A rummager intentionally sets out to buy every one of a specific item that can be found.*
- *A rummager suddenly realizes that he or she has accumulated a dozen or more of a particular object without having thought about it while buying.*

A classic illustration of how a collection begins is the rummager who purchased a tiny, ornate, Victorian-type picture frame containing a picture of an old-fashioned floral bouquet. It was not the type of treasure this rummager normally buys, but some unknown factor made the picture appealing. Soon, the buyer was searching for other similar treasures and buying all that could be found for "the new collection."

One fellow rummager confides that he collects almost anything he can lay his hands on, except phonograph records. A female rummager is proud of her collection of three hundred frogs in various sizes, colors and textures, and positions.

Need sometimes spawns collections. *Example:* One couple was not particularly interested in dolls. But, there were occasions when they needed certain types of dolls for specific uses. The need prompted a new interest in collecting dolls.

Curiosity creates collections. When rummagers notice an interesting object that comes in a variety of styles or sizes, they often become obsessed with how many "different aspects of the same" may be found in the series. *Example:* Coffee mugs shaped like Santa Claus heads have a variety of facial coloring and expressions.

Some collections may lose appeal because they require too much space to contain. For instance, you can only accommodate so many cookie jars before you run out of places to put them.

SECONDHAND GIFTS

The idea of using secondhand treasures for gifts is fantastic! Rummagers of all ages are boasting about the bargain buys they found for gifts and the "neat things" they have found for their friends' and relatives' collections. It's a great way to stretch the gift-giving budget.

Although it might be difficult to believe, there was a time before garage sales became popular when people were hesitant to buy secondhand merchandise for themselves, let alone as a gift, which was unthinkable! Now using secondhand treasures for gifts is the "in thing" to do.

People who receive secondhand treasures for gifts are lucky! These gifts can't be bought at just any place, any time. Much time and effort goes into finding them. Some, especially additions to collections, are searched for year-round. Many receivers of secondhand gifts appreciate them most because it shows the giver cares enough about their special interests to look for appropriate treasures.

Spending a quarter for a gift for a friend or relative might sound cheap. But, if that gift is an addition to a collection or a treasure which the recipient has been searching for, the "cheap" item might be highly treasured forever.

Create a gift pantry in your home. The location can be a shelf, a cupboard, a box, a table, or almost any place where gifts for relatives and friends can be stored until they are needed. When gifts are stored in a central location, it is easier to keep track of what you have and where it is as things accumulate during the year. The rummager who buys secondhand gifts for numerous people might want to take the "gift pantry" a step further and make individual storage boxes for each person's future gifts.

Treasure Hunter's Tips

SECONDHAND GIFT IDEAS

A new city map makes a nice and thoughtful little gift for an avid rummager.

Tins make multipurpose gifts. The collector of tins might enjoy receiving one filled with a food treat. They can also be used as gift boxes for small gifts.

Small flower planters, trinket boxes, and open figurines can be used as gift packages for small jewelry items — making two gifts in one, the package and the contents.

Attractive wicker baskets may be used for holding flowerpots — inventive gift packages for flower lovers.

Small items found in rummaging bargain boxes make great grab bag gifts for parties, or Christmas stocking stuffers.

Gag gifts — secondhand marketplaces are excellent sources of gag gifts for fun-loving rummagers.

A charming old candy dish bought for a quarter and filled with the recipient's favorite candy is always an appreciated gift.

Find unusual packaging such as an attractive flower planter shaped like a train engine to hold a Christmas gift of a large bag of M&Ms.

A short, large-mouthed bud vase is an excellent container for hard candy or artificial flowers.

A large vase purchased for a nominal fee, filled with fresh flowers from your garden, makes a great birthday gift.

A Christmas gift tip heard on the radio: The disc jockey advised shoppers to watch for teapots and sugar bowls without lids, cream pitchers, and mugs at garage sales and thrift stores. Even if slightly chipped on the inside, the containers can be used as flowerpots for small plants and given as gifts. African violets were especially recommended. Secondhand gift-giving must be a national trend!

For the nostalgic friend who is a popcorn lover, fill an old blue or green fruit jar with popcorn — a nice addition to a country kitchen decor.

Fruit jars also make nice candy gift containers for children of all ages — especially when the candy is licorice or jelly beans.

Tape record songs off old records for music lovers. Looking through records in search of special songs is a great rainy day project.

Old phonograph records of children's songs, stories, and rhymes can often be bought for 25¢. Make tape recordings as gifts for little friends. Add to the charm of the gift by including a stuffed animal or figurine to match a part of the record. *Example:* For a recording of Dr. Seuss's story *Horton Hears a Who,* include a stuffed elephant with the tape.

Buy used children's books and record them as you read out loud. The youngster hears the story in your own voice, which is especially nice for grandchildren. An added bonus is that many of the nickel and dime story books contain old, classic stories and rhymes seldom heard today.

A young mother told friends who are a rummaging couple that she was interested in a set of small Mickey and Minnie Mouse stuffed animals for her son. Because toys are collectible, the rummagers guessed that the toddler would not be allowed to play with them. So, when they found the toys, they gave them as a gift — to the mom!

A rummager gave her neighbors a gag gift of a

Cabbage Patch Doll puzzle that pictured the dolls making a garden. The couple decided to put the puzzle together, frame it, and present it to the former owner as a birthday present. When they discovered that one puzzle piece was missing, they had the clever idea of making a new piece — with a snapshot of the rummaging neighbor working in *her* garden on it! They removed two additional puzzle pieces, traced the opening to make a pattern, cut the snapshot of the rummager to fit, and glued it onto a piece of cardboard. When trimmed, the piece fit perfectly into the theme of the puzzle. The recipient was delighted!

Many beer mugs and glasses are attractive and collectible. Create a unique gift package containing a pair of glasses or mugs, a basket filled with mixed nuts in the shells, and red bandanna handkerchief napkins. Add a nut cracker and nut picks. Slip a five-dollar bill into one of the glasses with a note saying "For your favorite beverage." And, remember, the glasses don't have to be used for beer. Milk or soda pop is just as good in them.

One rummager gave a jar of home-canned hot dill pickles as a gift. For an added touch, she placed a stuffed monkey on the jar that had wires in the arms and legs which could be twisted around the jar. It gave the surprised recipients a laugh.

Secondhand Christmas decorations make great gifts. Give them as autumn birthday gifts or just "special friend" gifts a few weeks before Christmas, so they can be used as part of that year's decorating.

Part Two:

Caring For and Using Your Treasures

Like the bee, we should make our industry our amusement.

— Oliver Goldsmith

A dirty exterior is a great enemy to beauty of all descriptions.

— Mary Martha Sherwood, *The History of John Marten*

CHAPTER 3

CLEANING AND REPAIRING TREASURES

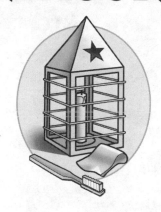

As much as rummagers would like them to be, not all second hand treasures are in perfect condition. Some just need cleaning; others need repair. Neither task has to be a costly venture.

Everyone has their own favorite cleaning supplies. Most of these can be used for cleaning treasures as well. There are also many staples found in any cupboard or medicine cabinet that can be used as cleaning agents.

An elaborate workshop and expensive tools are not necessary to do most treasure repairs. Simple, ordinary tools found in almost every home and household items that can substitute for tools are usually quite sufficient. Many repairs can be made at the kitchen table. Although a nice workshop area is handy, even a shabby old garage can be used for doing repair work.

SUPPLIES AND TOOLS

I keep the following supplies on hand for cleaning, painting, and repairing secondhand treasure. Brand names are optional, but the results may vary if you use others. Here are my recommendations for cleaning: Direct, Mr. Clean, Power (bought at a janitorial supply store), Clorox, white vinegar, brown vinegar, baking soda (wet and dry), cornstarch, peanut butter, rubbing alcohol, hair spray, fingernail polish remover, Brasso, Murphy's Oil Soap, Endust, Liquid Gold, and Parker's Lemon Oil.

USING YOUR COUNTY EXTENSION SERVICE

A good source of information on cleaning and repairing various surfaces is your county Cooperative Extension Service. Most states have this service, located in county-seat towns. The Extension office is linked to one of the state universities, and usually has a toll-free telephone number.

This service began in the agriculture field. It later expanded to supply farmers' wives with recipes and helpful hints about cleaning and fixing almost anything. The Cooperative Extension office is a mainstay of the 4-H program and 4-H county fairs.

The staff can supply you with many tips for cleaning items with everyday products (such as cornstarch) commonly stored in kitchen cupboards. Many users of the Extension service have commented that they really appreciate these methods because they are so much cheaper than buying a commercial cleaner that they aren't even certain will work.

While the Extension service is not allowed to recommend particular brand names, it will supply a list of several products having similar characteristics for a specific use. Example: When I called for a "home remedy" for cleaning brass, the Extension agent I spoke with also named three commercial cleaners that could be used for the task.

My tool list includes items used for securing treasures in display units and for constructing display areas in addition to those used for making repairs. Two tool groups need special attention: screwdrivers and brushes.

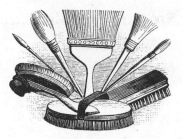

Collection of brushes

All rummagers should invest in screwdrivers. They come in a wide assortment of sizes and are sturdy and easy to use for *many* things. A good selection of styles and types of brushes — paint, tooth, fingernail, makeup, utility, vegetable, lint — also come in handy for cleaning and touch-up work. Toothbrushes with varying degrees of bristle stiffness are especially useful and economical. They can frequently be purchased on sale at discount stores for a quarter each. A good assortment of makeup brushes can often be found at a garage sale priced at a dime each. Q-Tips make good substitutes for small brushes.

Here are some other useful repair supplies to have on hand: nails (especially small ones), thumbtacks, screws, wire coat hangers, paper clips, bobby pins, bread and garbage bag twist-ties, wire hangers used for hanging Christmas ornaments, stiff wire, rubber bands, heavy string, yarn, masking tape, duct tape, silver tape, packing tape, adhesive tape, electrical tape, cellophane (Scotch), magnetic tape, Elmer's All-Purpose Glue, The Household Welder (glue), Weld Bond (glue), Elmer's Carpenter Woodfill (also patches figurines and ceramics), an eyelash curler to use as a clamp when gluing or working on small items, emery boards, various grades of sandpaper, rough washcloths, soft cloths, discarded electrical cords, Krylon spray paint, "Brush System 20:20 Brilliant Watercolor Brush/Pens" (pastel to bold shades work well on low-gloss ceramics), Testor's Paint Markers (look near the model kits in your toy department and buy a number of bold enamel colors), Apple Barrel paint (available in craft departments: goes on easily, easy-to-clean up waterbase, is a dream to work with, comes in a wide selection of colors), fingernail polish, Crayola Marker (good variety of colors in fine and wide line), and shoelaces.

Storing Supplies and Tools

When working on a treasure, it is convenient to have everything you need at your fingertips in one portable box of supplies. A shoebox makes a good storage case for small tools, emery boards, sandpaper, paints, and other small accessories.

A large supply and variety of paints are handier and more useful if they are organized and stored separately or in specific groupings. Cigar boxes, especially wooden ones, make great storage kits for this.

It is not always possible to find time to do touch-up and repair work immediately. Create storage boxes to keep tattered treasures in a central location where they will not be forgotten.

ORGANIZE YOUR REPAIR JOBS

I like to sort my treasures awaiting repairs so none are lost or forgotten. It also helps me to find the job I can do in the time I have — whenever that time arises! Two boxes work well for this purpose:

- *The Fix-It Box, for items that need major repairs or paint jobs.*
- *The Touch-Up Box, for objects that just need a little touch-up paint work or minor repairs.*

CLEANING TREASURES

Cleaning treasures is always an experiment! Old finishes, especially on figurines and Christmas tree ornaments, come off easily. Experienced antiques dealers and flea market vendors say this is because the dyes, paints, and methods of finishing in decades past are inferior to today's supplies and methods.

In many instances, cleaning is trial and error — so hope for the best. A cleaning agent that produces excellent results for one treasure might be disastrous for another. The risk of ruining finishes on both old and new items makes one hesitant to try out new products.

CLEANING SOLUTIONS

Household bleach disinfects glass, plastic, and most other surfaces. However, it is not recommended for wood or wicker.

Rubbing alcohol removes glue residue from high-gloss ceramics. *Example:* A sloppy repair job left obvious old glue residue on a rooster figurine. The glue was roughed up with an emery board and then gently wiped away with a soft cloth dampened with rubbing alcohol.

Hair spray can be used to remove marking pen prices from glass. Simply spray the mark and wipe away with a soft cloth or paper towel. Sometimes, more than one application is needed — especially on cut-glass treasures. Hair spray is also quite effective for removing glue residue left by masking tape. I've also heard hair spray sometimes removes ink from fabric, although I haven't had occasion to use it.

Endust removes marking pen ink. This hint was found by accident when a rummager happened to have a beer glass in one hand and a dustcloth treated with Endust in the other. The marking pen price mark on the bottom of the glass was wiped away with no effort when the rummager accidentally wiped the bottom of the glass with the cloth. Endust also removed a stubborn marking pen price mark from the bottom of a tin, but several applications were needed.

A damp cloth dipped in dry baking soda sometimes removes ink or crayon marks from walls or other surfaces.

Lemon oil is impressive. It is not destructive to old finishes like some cleaners are. In fact, it seems to be a restorative. It works well on old and new finishes, ceramics, plastics, and wood. The oil does *not* work well on clear glass, where it creates a greasy appearance. My first experiment with lemon oil: I cleaned a brand new ceramic clown bank and an aged apple pencil holder with it. Both treasures gleamed, and the apple looked as new as the clown. After two weeks, both treasures still had such a gleam that they looked as if they had just been cleaned. And when I applied lemon oil to some low-gloss figurines of birds, the colors were enhanced to rich, glowing deep shades.

Liquid Gold can be used on plastic, ceramic, and wooden treasures. It transformed the dull finish of a low-gloss, mallard duck planter to a rich, mellow glow. Many glass and ceramic treasures have a better sheen when cleaned with Liquid Gold than with glass cleaners. Liquid Gold also frequently conceals tattered marks and worn surfaces of wooden knickknacks and candle pedestals. Use Liquid Gold on cookie jars and canisters as well, and to clean and shine miniature brass kitchen utensils in a shadow box.

Brasso works well for cleaning copper and brass treasures. My county Extension Service also offers the following home remedies for cleaning brass: Wash object, and rinse thoroughly. Make a paste by combining one tablespoon flour, one tablespoon salt, and one tablespoon white vinegar. Scrub the treasure with the paste and rinse thoroughly.

Or, dip a cut lemon in salt and rub the brass surface. Again, rinse thoroughly.

The Extension agent stressed the importance of thorough rinsing for both of these techniques. Failure to rinse well allows the acid from the vinegar or lemon to eat into the metal. White vinegar is recommended because the sugar in cider vinegar has an adverse effect on the cleaning process.

Peanut butter will remove tape residue from smooth surfaces, such as a copper wall plaque. With bare fingertips, rub a small amount of peanut butter over the surface. Wipe away with a paper towel, and repeat the procedure. My results: The glue disappears, and the surface is polished to a high sheen.

Cider vinegar works well for pots and pans with rust. Rinse with cider vinegar, pour out vinegar, let pans stand a few days, and the rust should disappear. The same procedure may also work on tins, which are sometimes too interesting to resist even though marred by a small amount of rust inside. Even with rust marks inside, however, tins can still be used to hold food gifts. Just wash thoroughly and line with waxed paper, or foil.

Soap and water works well on baskets. This no-pains-taken, quick-cleaning method is surprisingly satisfactory: Swish baskets in a sink filled with rich suds; use a stiff-bristled utility brush to remove stubborn patches of soil; rinse baskets immediately with cool water and shake to remove excess water. Store in a large paper bag until dry.

Glass Plus works well on baskets that don't need a thorough cleaning, but they do need to be spruced up a bit. Spray on and wipe with a soft cloth for a nice, clean shine. A small paint brush works well for general basket dusting.

Soap suds and a stiff vegetable brush work well for cleaning stuffed animals with short pile, and a toothbrush is good for small areas around the eyes and in the ears. Work with the nap and then against it, and blot the animal with paper towels. It will dry quickly; fluff it with your hands to help. A brush does not work well on animals with longer pile or loops. Instead, use a coarse washcloth.

Cornstarch works for dry cleaning stuffed animals. Rub into pile and let stand overnight. Take animal outside and shake out loose cornstarch. Brush with a stiff brush. The result is clean, fresh, fluffy toys.

The cornstarch dry cleaning method also works well on pile trim and white yarn hair common on Mr. and Mrs. Santa Claus and craft figures of old men and women.

When you don't know what materials or substances are in the treasure, proceed cautiously. I cleaned a small old dog figurine that had a chalky surface by com-bining a small amount of warm water with a good quantity of liquid dish soap to form rich suds. Using a soft-bristled toothbrush to scoop up as much suds with as little water as possible, I brushed the dog with quick, gentle strokes, blotted it dry, and left it to finish drying naturally. Re-gardless of the price paid for a treasure, a rummager never wants it to be ruined by cleaning techniques which fail. As with the little dog which only cost a nickel, many of the least expensive treasures are the most charming or interesting. In this instance, the cleaning effort was totally successful.

Whenever using the soap suds method described above for surface cleaning treasures, the rule of thumb is as much suds and as little water as possible. Shampoo, laundry soap, and dish soap can all be used. Dish soap bubbles nicely, is gentle, cleans most surfaces, and, if rinsing is desired, it doesn't require much.

It often works better to mix a small quantity of suds in a large bowl or a small pail instead of making a sinkful. Large quantities of suds tend to drop quickly, whereas smaller amounts tend to produce more suds and last longer. Besides, it is no trouble to mix up a fresh batch if more suds are needed.

Small vases, figurines, and trinket boxes decorated with delicate, sculpted roses are some of the most difficult treasures to clean because the flowers break

easily and many of the surfaces are made of porous materials. There is no way to guarantee successful cleaning of porous surfaces. Sometimes, these treasures come out looking like new; others crumble in your hands or are discolored by cleaning solutions. Again, try the soap suds method. Apply suds with extremely soft bristles, and work quickly! Rinse and dry immediately. *Note:* Use a small paint brush or makeup brush for dusting flowers and other delicate features of figurines during general cleaning.

For cleaning alabaster owl and dove figurines, my county Extension Service supplied two home remedies: 1) Rub the figures with a generous amount of cornstarch; let stand for several hours before brushing cornstarch away with a soft brush. 2) Wipe with a damp (not soaking) cloth. Use only clear water because detergents tend to cause discoloration. **Note:** Water can destroy alabaster-composition figurines.

Hard-to-Clean Surfaces

Felt items are extremely difficult to clean because they fade. In some instances, the soap suds method has been successful, but there is still no guarantee the item will not be ruined. I've also used corn-

CLEANING CHRISTMAS BALLS

It is a common reaction to look at an old Christmas tree ornament and think, "This is dirty. I need to clean it." And, they do look so pretty when they are clean. But Christmas tree balls are some of the most difficult treasures to clean because the finish comes off so easily. Balls having traces of artificial snow on them tend to peel even more than those that don't.

Never attempt to clean a Christmas tree decoration you are extremely fond of or that you know is an antique. It is better to have it dirty than to run the risk of ruining it.

If you do want to attempt cleaning Christmas balls, wiping with a damp (not soaking) cloth may work. Use only clear water and no cleaning substances. Regardless of how careful the cleaning technique, there is always a high risk the finish will come off the balls. My personal experience is that red balls peel more than blue balls. Most balls have a silver finish under the surface color, so they can still be used if all colored paint is removed.

Clean Christmas ornaments as far in advance of Christmas as possible to allow plenty of time to find replacements if they are ruined during cleaning. If discarding damaged ornaments, save the caps and hanging wires to use as replacement parts for others.

starch dry cleaning on felt items, but it should only be attempted on very durable items because much brushing is required to remove the cornstarch from bright colors.

Secondhand plastic toys such as building blocks, which have most certainly been in the mouths of children, should be disinfected in a nontoxic way. My county Extension Office recommends mixing two tablespoons household bleach with one gallon water. This mixture is potent enough to sanitize toys, while its toxicity will dissipate into the air with no cause for concern. One young mother I know was delighted with this safe, simple tip that eliminates the need to purchase high-priced cleaners.

Removing Candle Wax

Removing candle wax is always a problem! Use caution when removing partial candles from glass votive candle holders because the glass can break while you're working. Protect your hands with gloves or oven mitts; at the very least, wrap a towel around the candle holder while working. Light the candle to soften the wax, but don't let it get too hot. Insert a thin screwdriver blade next to the wick and twist. Soft textured candles pop out in one piece and are easily removed; hard textured candles break apart and come out in chunks.

A paring knife can also be used for removing wax, but a screwdriver works better since it's sturdier, safer, and easier to handle. There is also less danger of the blade breaking, and a screwdriver doesn't have to be disinfected after using.

Wax can also be softened slowly by setting the candle holder on a steam radiator or over the pilot light of a gas range, or by filling the candle holder with hot water and letting it stand a while before prying the wax loose. This method is the least desirable and least effective.

If an occasion arises when a cleaning technique is a total failure and a treasure is ruined, salvage any useable parts — such as buckles, buttons, bows, bells, or moving eyes — that could be used for repairing other items.

Basic Treasure Repair Advice

It is sometimes more difficult to find time for tiny repairs taking only a few minutes than for larger, time-consuming repairs. Simple solutions are sometimes slower to come to mind because we have a tendency to search too hard for answers — and put off the work.

Putting off doing small repairs leads to bulky build-up of objects in your fix-it boxes. It also increases the amount of time needed to do the work.

These procedures work for removing wax from containers that weren't designed to be candle holders as well. Many people have a passion for making their own candles by pouring wax into anything from a delicate wine glass to a coffee mug. Be extra cautious when removing wax from these containers. They were not made to withstand the heating and cooling effects produced by candle use.

After the main candle body is removed from the holder, tiny wax particles sometimes cling to interior crevices and indentations. Fill the container with a mixture of hot water and household bleach. Let stand for several hours to remove particles. Wash; repeat soaking procedure, if desired.

Tapered candle stubs can be removed easily by inserting a screwdriver blade next to the wick and twisting.

Murphy's Oil Soap works well for removing candle drippings from wooden candle holders. Polish with Liquid Gold.

To remove wax drippings from silver candle holders, place candle holders in freezer. When wax hardens, it will easily peel off without harming the silver surface..

Remember, some flaws don't have to be repaired. Sometimes they contribute to the effect of rustic treasures. *Example:* A trio of gaudy pictures of wildlife scenes were in tattered old frames. The rummager's first inclination was to paint the frames, but then decided against it when he realized how much character and rustic charm the frames added.

Adding a New Coat of Paint

A coat of paint can cover a multitude of sins and render an entirely new appearance. Unfortunately, weather conditions can delay paint work.

An experienced flea market vendor advises that when old paint is peeling off figurines, strip away the remainder of the paint by running the figurine through a cycle in an automatic dishwasher. The treasure is then ready to be repainted.

Touch-up work on old figurines frequently improves their appearances, but it detracts from the charm of age. Yesteryear's theory was that touch-up work decreased the value of old treasures. However, today, many vendors are repainting before selling. This is one example of what you see is *not* what you get!

In the region where I live, there are many old, red-painted compotes circulating. No one seems to remember much about them or even when they were popular, but their availability and low prices means they are not collectible. Moreover, most of them have peeling paint which detracts from their appearance. However, once the paint is removed, a lovely, clear glass bowl is revealed.

Treasure Hunter's Tips

PAINTING TREASURES

When using paint pens, be certain the paint is dry before switching to a different color or you'll ruin the tip of the next marker used.

A little repair work and a fresh coat of paint can make a big difference in covering up flaws. I had a set of dog-shaped salt and pepper shakers, one of which needed only a little touch-up with a red paint marker. The other shaker needed more work: a chip in one ear needed sanding with an emery board and painting with a black paint marker; old glue residue from a previous repair needed sanding as well.

When new paint was finally applied, the flaw was concealed and the shaker took on an appealing new look.

I also had an aged pheasant figurine that had two long, shallow chips on the underside of its tail. Once smoothed with an emery board, and colored with a low-gloss, watercolor paint pen, the chips became invisible.

When paint color for touch-up work on a multicolor treasure can't be matched, use a contrasting color. *Example:* A chocolate brown and burnt orange rooster-shaped cookie jar had several small chips. The chips were sanded with an emery board, filled with wood putty, and smoothed with fine sandpaper. The brown Testor's paint marker did not match the brown of the cookie jar, but the orange pen made an excellent accent touch-up color.

When purchasing unpainted ceramic figurines, protect them from dirt by spray painting them white until you have time for finer painting work. Spray low-gloss figurines, especially handmade ceramics, with a coat of clear Krylon to make them easier to clean.

Spray gold, key-shaped wall plaques with a light overcoat of black paint for a charming "antiqued" look.

When a crack is still noticeable after a treasure has been repaired but you just can't bring yourself to throw it away, you may be able to salvage it by concealing the flaw with matching paint (or perhaps a ribbon), or alternatively, highlight the flaw with a contrasting paint color.

You may buy some treasures for a specific feature — such as the fancy handle on a beer stein or the unique shape of a vase — but find the color unappealing. Just spray paint the treasure to make it fit your color scheme or taste. Spray paint also works well on wrought iron.

When I found it impossible to remove a stain from the cloth face of a clown doll, I painted the entire face with a Crayola Marker.

One rummager I know had the following "problem" treasure: A cut-glass goblet with an interesting pattern, but a dull finish with absolutely no sparkle. The glass felt chalky, but no trace of any type of residue was detectable and none of the cleaning methods worked. The solution: Spray paint it black and make it into an interesting, functional treasure.

Another rummager was in search of a belt to wear with a Santa Claus suit. The secondhand belt found was the right style, but the wrong color. Two solutions: 1) The belt could be painted black; or 2) Black satin ribbon could be glued onto the belt.

Brown liquid shoe polish works well in some cases for staining wood or covering flaws in wooden treasures.

Gluing Treasures

One of the challenges of gluing is finding a good place to leave things to dry. For small, quick repairs of items that are simply left to sit until dry, place them on waxed paper. They are less apt to stick to the surface. If need be, the wax paper can easily be peeled away.

Old electrical cords work well for holding large items in place while glue is drying. For smaller items, try setting them in modeling clay until dry.

Store glue sticks, as well as bottles and tubes of glue, in a glass peanut butter, salad dressing, or fruit jar. This way, even if the tops of the glue containers are not completely closed, the airtight glass jar will prevent them from drying out. An added bonus is that all your glue is kept together.

Weld Bond is an excellent glue. It comes in a tube and has the texture of Elmer's glue. The directions say it dries in an hour, but many textures bond in just minutes. I've used it successfully to repair such items as a flower planter and a Hall pottery vase.

Record album jackets can be repaired with tape without detracting from their collectible value. Glue any loose seams.

Sometimes you can glue a broken piece of glass or ceramic on seamlessly. Other times a chip or nick in a cut-glass or ceramic piece can be sanded smooth — you may be able to even eliminate it entirely. Even if the nick can still be felt, there will no longer be jagged edges to cut fingers on during cleaning.

Repairing Chipped or Nicked Treasures

Large or extremely rough chips should first be sanded with fine sandpaper. If needed, this can be refined by smoothing with an emery board. Many tiny chips need only an emery board. I had an emerald green Fenton cut-glass shoe figurine with a small, but jagged and noticeable, chip near the toe. After smoothing with both sandpaper and an emery board, I showed the shoe to an experienced rummager who collects shoes. She could not find the location of the flaw! I did the same with a ceramic figurine of an elf that had a small chip in a prominent place. After sanding with an emery board, and touching up with a paint marker, the flaw went undetected by a very experienced, expert rummager. In the instance of a small amber-colored relish tray, however, the chips were too deep to be eliminated. But sanding made the flaws less unattractive and the dish safe to use.

To repair a chip beneath the handle of a white ceramic beer stein, I filled it with Elmer's Woodfill, allowed it to dry for twenty-four hours, and then sanded the filler and painted it with a paint marker. This method of patching produced satisfactory results. My only problem was that the paint I used was too white — the body of the stein looked cream-colored in comparison.

Sanding pottery is *not* recommended: it crumbles! Some chips in pottery can be filled with wood fill, but use extreme caution to ensure you sand only the filler. Sometimes, just a little touch-up paint will conceal pottery flaws. Handle pottery with extreme care! It breaks easily, and it appears to be more fragile than many types of glass.

Treasure Hunter's Tips

REPAIRING AND RESTORING

Many figurines of people, especially children, have their hands in positions that indicate they were holding something: The holes where the missing objects fit are quite obvious. Conceal these by giving the character something to hold. *Examples:* For a lady or girl figure who looks as if she once carried an umbrella or held a broom, place a very tiny flower in the hole. Or, buy a package of those little umbrellas used in some alcoholic drinks and slip the stick of one in the hole.

For the little boy figurines who once held fishing poles, make new ones: Stick a toothpick into the hole in the hands, attach a piece of light string or thread to the other end of the toothpick, and make a wire "fishhook" to fasten to the end of the string. Miniature flags can be added to almost any figurine.

Banks are frequently missing bottom stoppers. Repair by covering the hole with packing tape, finding a cork that fits, or taking a stopper from the bottom of another bank. If you find them cheaply, buy miscellaneous banks and save the stoppers just to use in banks you like.

Broken pieces of jewelry, such as brooches without clasps, earrings without backs, or necklace fobs without hanging loops, should not be discarded. Use pearls, rhinestones, or other settings from these pieces as replacement stones for usable jewelry.

Some filigree-bell Christmas ornaments have sizable holes in their tops and no hanging wires. For easy hanging, slip a mini Christmas tree ball into the bell so its hanging loop protrudes through the opening in the bell and attach a hanging wire.

Many nonworking music boxes can be repaired simply by removing the music box mechanism from the casing, spraying it with WD-40, and reinserting it in the box.

Interchange parts: You may buy some objects solely for the purpose of using their parts in other treasures. *Example:* The parts from an old wooden picture frame with glass in it, but missing the piece on the back used to set the frame up for display, can be used to complete a gold frame of the same size that is missing glass, but has the back section in tact.

Some decorative plates come with their own installed hanging loops, but these sometimes come loose, allowing the plates to fall and break. The hangers should be reinforced with tape, or the plates should be placed in wire plate hangers.

Plastic placemats that have been rolled up for a long time will not lie flat. This can be corrected by washing the placemats in hot water and laying them flat to dry.

One rummager acquired a basket shaped like a fish, but the handle that arched over the top was broken in the center. The break was taped with packing tape and a red, felt bow with a gold wire was attached to conceal the tape.

On old china dishes, several antiques dealers have advised me not to attempt to remove the tiny lines because they are age indicators.

Greeting card pictures make attractive refrigerator magnets. Glue them into the lids of small throw-away bottles and affix magnetic tape to the back.

Rolls of wallpaper can sometimes be found at garage sales at prices ranging from a dime to a dollar per roll. Wallpaper is extremely versatile. Use it to cover lampshades, boxes, old jewelry cases, picture frames, and many more things. It also makes great shelf paper.

Magazine advertisements and pictures and old calendars also make great picture frame fillers.

To restore picture frames: Replace torn or missing dust covers on the back with pretty wrapping paper; spray paint both metal and wooden picture frames; cover tattered frames with attractive fabrics to conceal flaws.

NEW USES FOR OLD GREETING CARDS

Greeting cards can be converted into excellent pictures for empty or hard-to-fit frames. Cards frequently appear in bulk quantities at garage sales with prices averaging one or two cents per card. Individual pictures or sections of cards can be successfully cut to fit small frames.

One example is a neat, aged, wooden frame with a gold inner edge that had neither a glass nor a backing. The frame was also an odd size that made it difficult to find a picture to fit. I found a deep red valentine with gold, dusty rose, and muted avocado accents that fit perfectly into the frame. The frame and valentine combined to create a charming, old-fashioned, rustic picture.

Do not cut individual pictures or small sections of cards until they are needed. It is impossible to predict exactly which sizes will be needed at later dates. To store large quantities of cards for later use, cut away the backs and any useless sections to reduce the bulk.

Floppy ears on some stuffed elephants and Mickey Mouse characters fall forward over the face. A straight pin works well for a quick repair. Insert the pin from the back side, catch the material, and return the tip to insert in the head behind the ear. This hint is for display only; it can't be used on toys that children will be playing with! For a more permanent repair that is safe for children, tack the ears back by sewing.

Instead of gluing or sewing new replacement eyes on stuffed animals, consider drawing eyes with a permanent marker or a Crayola marker. Some of these freeform eyes are more attractive than the standard styles.

Use your imagination! A two-feet-tall stuffed monkey that had been dressed in a jogging suit had a small tear in one leg. The hole could have been repaired by sewing or gluing, but instead I covered it with an adhesive bandage, adding to the monkey's character.

Replace tattered or missing strings on pull toys with shoelaces. If the end of the lace is too large to work into the toy's loop, cut it off. Then, cut the lace in half lengthwise for about two inches. Use a wire hook or crochet hook to pull one half through the loop and tie securely to the other half. An added bonus of this replacement is that shoelaces are frequently easier for tiny tots to hold onto than the original string.

Missing rings on the ends of pull-toy strings can be replaced with a thread spool, a large washer, a large button, or a key. Be sure to use an item that is too large to swallow and to affix it securely.

CHAPTER 4

STORING TREASURES

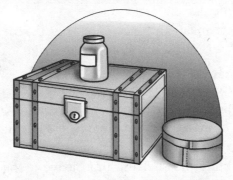

Unless rummagers are deliberately buying many treasures for resale, their beginning interests in rummaging are usually casual. They buy a few items here and there. Purchases are usually limited to additions to collections, things that contribute to decorating schemes, and treasures that just happen to catch the buyer's eye or fill a specific need.

As a rummager's interest — and involvement — grows, the quantity of purchases mushrooms. He or she will find themselves filling boxes, closets, cupboard shelves, and any available nook and cranny with newfound treasures. Eventually, the collection of treasures outgrows available storage space.

It is torture when an avid rummager who collects a wide variety of treasures has to pass up really neat items with reasonable prices because there is simply no room for them at home. Some rummagers expand their storage area by building shelving units in their basements or garages. A large, unused walk-in clothes closet is a great place to store treasures.

The ideal situation is to have a spare room — a bedroom or a porch not being used for something else — where treasures can be stored. The rummager who has a treasure room is, indeed, a lucky person. Such a domain never ceases to be fascinating, relaxing, enjoyable, and interesting. It is also a popular place, almost taking on the feeling of a tourist attraction when guests ask to visit it.

The phrase "out of sight, out of mind" applies to all treasures. Hidden away in boxes and cupboards, treasures are not utilized to their fullest potential. Treasures stored in visible locations are more accessible, less likely to break, and can be enjoyed as part of the decorating scheme.

Metal shelving units can be bought very inexpensively on sale at discount lumber/hardware stores that make excellent storage units for treasures, especially breakable ones. A four-shelf unit is a good size because the contents of each shelf are easily visible and within reach. Shelves twelve inches deep are better than those eighteen inches or more because there is less chance of small items being pushed to the rear and forgotten.

When assembling the shelving unit, leave a space beneath the bottom shelf so the floor space serves as an extra shelf — a good place for larger items like cookie jars and canisters. Install the shelves upside-down and you'll create a one-inch-deep edge to protect treasures from sliding or being pushed off the shelves.

Every rummager has his or her own favorite storage system. One system is the color code method: All the brown items on one shelf, only orange ones on another, and so on. Or, you could put related colors together, such as a section of shelves with just autumn-colored pieces. Another system is to organize by size, with small treasures separated from large ones.

STORAGE IDEAS

Use vases and bottles as storage containers for bouquets of artificial flowers. Set them at the rear of the top shelves so they don't block your view of shorter treasures. They also help decorate the storage room.

Hang whatnot shelves that are not being used for decorating purposes in the treasure room to use for storage.

Storage shelves double as decorating units when filled with interesting treasures and placed in various areas of the home.

Hanging treasures helps you review at a glance what you have on hand. Many small pictures, plaques, and mirrors can be easily hung on walls. Sometimes, in hanging items for storage that aren't normally grouped together side-by-side, you'll discover new and original decorating ideas.

Baskets should always be hung to protect them from being forgotten or damaged, which often happens when they're stuffed into storage boxes. They can be hung on small nails or wooden peg racks, or you can make your own loops by stringing a length of heavy string through open basket weave and securing it with a clothespin. Bend a paper clip open to use as a hanger, or use a wire designed for hanging Christmas tree ornaments.

In a treasure room, you can stretch heavy string or clothesline across the ceiling and suspend baskets from it. Baskets can also be hung on wire coat hangers suspended from the ceiling or hung on a wall.

Plastic clothes drying racks designed to fold out and hang over a bathtub (equipped with sturdy, firm-gripping mini clothespins) are also effective for hanging baskets. Suspend the rack from a hook in the ceiling of your treasure room.

Whatever method you choose for hanging baskets is sure to improve the appearance of your storage room, and free up floor and shelf space for items that can't be hung.

Use expandable wooden peg racks to their full potential. They can usually be hung with two nails, and have ten wooden pegs that can accommodate many treasures, especially if more than one is hung on each peg. Beer steins, mugs, and baskets store well on peg racks.

Some other, more unusual, possibilities include: high quality, clear glass beer mugs; decorative key rings; wrought iron candle sconces; sachet containers; and long-handled salt and pepper shakers with hanging loops.

Boxes are not recommended for storage because the "out of sight, out of mind" theory applies so strongly to all treasures. But, sometimes a rummager has no choice in the matter: Boxes are needed. Check with your local copy shops and office supply stores to find copy paper boxes, which make ideal storage boxes. They are large enough to contain a good number of treasures, but small enough to be easy to handle. They're also sturdy, have fit-on lids, and can be stacked to save floor space.

Save all old socks. They're great for wrapping treasures and guarding against breakage because they have a lot of "give." Socks fit over many items you wouldn't expect. *Example:* A six-inch diameter candle holder with a loop handle was protected by a man's sock.

For double protection, slip the treasure into the foot section of the sock, twist the top close to the treasure, and pull it down over the contents. Socks of all sizes — from the tiniest infants' through the largest men's — can be used to accommodate all sizes of treasures.

Store socks that aren't being used in a gym duffel bag, available for a quarter or less in a secondhand marketplace. The bag is easy to move around and pliable enough to be crammed into small storage places.

Storing treasures in boxes does have one rather unusual advantage: When seasonal items, such as Christmas objects, are bought several weeks or months in advance and stored in boxes for future use, it is fun to find them all over again when you unpack — like opening Christmas presents!

If you accumulate large quantities of candle holders and votive candles, you'll need a storage box just to hold them

ESSENTIAL STORAGE BOXES

B*oxes are not recommended when you can find an alternative, but every rummager has several storage boxes that are essential to keeping their treasures in order.*

The Just-What-I-Need Box contains a collection of small items that could easily be lost in the shuffle when stored with large objects. This box contains treasures a rummager has no immediate plans to use. On the other hand, one of these tiny treasures is sure to become "just what I need" when you aren't exactly certain what you're looking for.

The Someday Box provides a place for a rummager to store the numerous unwanted or even unliked objects purchased in a bargain box that had just one desirable treasure. There is usually absolutely nothing wrong with many of the other treasures, so they need to be stored until a future use is determined or they can be used as gifts — someday!

The Junk Box does not hold throwaway junk. Instead, it contains objects the rummager has no immediate plans for, that have no apparent function or are being saved to be taken apart for pieces. One never knows when such a box will yield exactly what is needed for a repair job.

The Ugly Candle Box is for unattractive candles that you wouldn't ordinarily buy but you just happen to have gotten along with candle holders or other treasures. These may come in handy for testing experimental lighting or in case of a power failure.

The Christmas Decorations Box is essential for holiday-celebrating rummagers. Store your accumulation of good-quality secondhand decorations here in one easy-to-find place.

because they take up too much valuable shelf storage space. To prevent breakage, individually wrap each piece and candle before putting in one large storage box. Unfortunately, this also discourages use because you have to unwrap many to find the one you're looking for — a time-consuming task.

You can solve this problem by layering the candle holders in the sturdy, shallow cardboard boxes made to transport cans of soft drinks, then placing these in a copy paper box. Begin by covering the bottom of the copy paper box with some of the least-used candle holders. Then fill a shallow box with unusual candle holders and set it on top of the foundation layer. Fill another box with common, everyday candle holders and set it in place. Obviously, this system works best when the objects in each layer are the same height so additional layers will be balanced.

This is an excellent storage system, since it's easy to lift out layers to find what's needed. And the box is a convenient size that can either be stacked or shoved into out-of-the-way floor space under a storage table. Leave your most attractive, unusual, and functional candle holders on the shelves.

The box layering storage system described previously can easily be adapted to hold wall hangings as well. Many rummagers tend to collect small pictures, frames, wall plaques, and mirrors. When you have too many of these treasures to hang on walls, the temptation is to stuff them, at random, into open storage boxes wherever space is available. These treasures are then more likely to be broken or scuffed, and they get in the way when you're looking for other items in the boxes. There is also the danger of breaking treasures or cutting hands.

It works well to use the box layer method and separate pictures and plaques into categories — seasonal, nostalgic, plaques with sayings written on them, wrought iron, or mirrors. Materials can also be separated by themes such as nautical or railroad pictures. Simply layer the wall hangings the same way as the candle holders were arranged. It makes them easy to find and you'll save time when you have to look for something because you can go to the box containing the category you're after.

Large automobile air filter boxes make great storage compartments for record albums.

Many electric blankets come packaged in clear, heavy-

STORING CUMBERSOME COOKIE JARS

Cookie jars are also a nuisance to store because they require ample storage space. If you are lucky enough to have the type of kitchen cupboards with display space on top, the cookie jar dilemma is over. Not only are they on display on cupboard tops, but they aren't taking up storage space elsewhere.

If you grow tired of a cookie jar display and want a change, simply move the jars to the back of the cupboard top and place large attractive pictures in front of them to conceal the jars. This produces an art gallery effect. A piece of double tape or modeling clay on the lower edges of the picture frames helps prevent slippage.

duty plastic zippered bags. These are some of the best storage units available! They're durable, hold many small treasures, keep contents clean, and, because they are transparent, make contents easy to find when needed. These bags are especially great for storing small dolls and stuffed animals and protecting collectible animals.

Package small items in high-quality zip-seal storage bags. Don't discard them; reuse them to store your own tiny treasures. This is a garage sale bonus — a free storage bag with purchase.

Popular collectible decorative tins are a nuisance to store when they aren't on display be-

cause they take up a lot of space and are easily dented or scratched. You can solve the problem this way: Use pieces of newspaper as protective dividers between the tins; stack them in a plastic grocery bag; slip the bag's loop handles over the hook of a coat hanger; and hang on an out-of-the-way rod in a closet.

When buying a new kitchen dish drainer, don't throw the old one away. Use it for storing picture frames, record albums, or decorative plates when not in use.

I saw an antiques dealer at a fair transporting her valuable decorator plates in plastic pails with lids — the kind that contain large quantities of ice cream or deli salads. This is a good idea for home storage of plates when not in use.

A folded-up rollaway bed yields valuable storage space. Extra blankets and afghans can be draped over the bed. An old coffee table top or a piece of wood can be placed on top of the bed to create a storage shelf for treasures, and floor space beneath the bed can also be used for storage.

When storing old salt shakers with metal lids, remove all salt before storing — it damages the lids.

CHAPTER 5

DISPLAYING AND USING YOUR TREASURES

The homes of avid rummagers are not normal. They are show-cases, with a museum air about them.

The reactions of visitors to rummagers' homes are fun, delight-ful, interesting, and, sometimes, amusing. Many visitors are curious and are not shy about looking around. They want to see every-thing. Some visitors can't resist the temptation to ask what treasures are, where they were bought, and even how much they cost. Then, there are visitors who are embarrassed about showing their curios-ity. They want to look around in the worst way, but they don't want to be obvious, so they sneak peeks.

It is especially rewarding when fellow rummagers are impressed by your collection. It is, indeed, a compliment when friends come to visit and admit they just came "to see all of the neat stuff."

Visitors who are non-rummagers and who, evidently, don't have any friends who are rummagers, are literally speechless when they walk into a rummager's home. I've seen people actually stand with their mouths hanging open — prompting me to look around and realize what a menagerie my home has become.

Rummagers who enjoy and use their treasures are praised for their creativity and imagination. It is rewarding to know your efforts and treasures are appreciated. Rummagers put much time and work into their decorating, but they have fun doing it. It is even more fun when visitors enjoy what they see. Rummagers are flattered by such remarks as the following: "Your home is almost like a museum," or, "This is the kind of place that makes visitors want to buy things right off the walls and shelves," or, "I like to visit here because I never change my decor at home, and you always have something different," or "You have so many neat things!"

DEVELOPING ORIGINAL DECOR

Don't be afraid to be original. People grow accustomed to and anticipate the "unusual" from rummagers. Friends, relatives, and fellow rummagers expect rummagers to continually have new treasures and new ideas.

Visitors accept your quaintness. Guests don't ask why there are heavy strings draped across the kitchen ceiling, why there is a toy blimp suspended from that ceiling, or why there is a Sesame Street dart board in the living room of a home where the children are all grown. And, in a rummager's home, it seems perfectly normal to see stuffed animals being treated like pieces of sculpture or an artificial Christmas tree on top of the refrigerator decorated with miniature flags in July.

So, let your imagination go. Don't be afraid to combine unique and old treasures to create an interesting, museumlike effect. Put one-of-a-kind items in ordinary places and do unusual things with ordinary treasures. This is trial-and-error decorating. What you may visualize as being perfect doesn't always work out. Experiment! Move things around.

Some of the most interesting and attractive decorating schemes come about by accident. *Examples:* Setting a beer stein on an out-of-the-way end table until there is time to put it away, and then discovering that's just the touch the room needed. Or,

Wooden rocking horse

plopping a bouquet of flowers in a bottle and realizing the two are a perfect pair.

Sometimes, it only takes setting a single treasure in an unusual place to add just the touch needed. *Example:* A wooden toy horse set beside a French door was perfect in the country kitchen of an old home. But, it often takes time to put a decorating scheme together. Treasures are bought one at a time from different second-hand marketplaces. How well such pieces coordinate is amazing.

There is no excuse for a rummager to be bored with his or her decor. Use treasures! Change accessories frequently; be daring and unpredictable; and have fun! The more you enjoy yourself, the better the effect will be.

Keep track of what you've done. Photograph your displays. It is nice to reflect on what was where when. Pictures may prompt future decorating ideas.

CREATING DISPLAY SPACE

One of the first concerns of rummagers is where to display treasures. There never seems to be enough shelf and wall space. Improvise and use what you have.

Windows

Why do you have curtains and draperies? Is the reason for privacy or to decorate your home? If the answer is decorating, consider getting rid of them. Mini-blinds and valances are popular alternatives. Think about going one step further and using plain white window shades. Leave the bar curtain rods in place to use as decorating aids. Treasures can be hung from the rods or set on top of them. *Examples:* Collections of stuffed animals and dolls can be placed in hanging plant baskets and suspended from the curtain rods. The white shade makes an excellent background. Stuffed animals or dolls can also be set on top of the rods and secured with light wire, heavy string, or garbage bag twist-ties.

The absence of long curtains also frees windowsills for displaying figurines and other treasures. This is a great decorating aid — especially if you live in a home where the windows are closed all year long or, at least, during the winter months.

Casings over windows, doorways, and arches are built-in display areas. This is particularly true in older homes where such woodwork is often two to four inches wide.

Shelving

Many kitchens have at least eighteen inches between the tops of the cupboards and the ceiling. This is valuable decorating space! It can accommodate larger items and add interesting decorating touches to your kitchen.

Small decorative wooden shelves are popular for country-style decorating and displaying miniatures. They may range from $4 to $25 in price and can support either one large treasure or a collection of several tiny miniatures.

Wrought iron candle sconces for pillar candles have platforms two to three inches in diameter that make great display shelves for one large or several small treasures. Just bend down the decorative metal prongs around the outside edges to allow space for a larger treasure, and then bend back up to hold it in place. If need be, the sconces can be painted with spray paint.

These sconces can usually be found in secondhand marketplaces priced from 25¢ to 50¢. But they aren't always available, so buy them when you find them and store for future use.

Wooden candle sconces with platforms are more difficult to find, and are usually more expensive. They are attractive and produce a different look than the wrought iron ones, but the absence of prongs places restrictions on what can be displayed.

If you are ever lucky enough to find old-fashioned, wooden kitchen chairs with intricately carved tops on the backs, snatch them up — even if the rest of the chair is in poor condition. The backs can be cut away from the chairs and transformed into lovely display shelves. At flea markets, I've seen these backs placed on top of the rear side of a piece of wood to form the shelf back. There is only one thing wrong with this idea — when treasures are put on the shelf, the decorative back is hidden, especially when the shelf is hung high up. So, why not turn the chair back upside down and use the decorative design as the exterior bottom of a shelf?

As mentioned on page 93, spice racks are easily converted into whatnot shelves. Although they are scarce, old-fashioned wooden whatnot shelves, consisting of one shelf with a decorative back, can sometimes be found. Consider hanging such a shelf upside-down so the attractive, decorative top hangs down against the wall and is more visible. The bottom of the shelf is as functional a display area as the top.

Old bunk bed ladders also make unique display shelves. They are usually composed of quality wood and have a finish that coordinates with almost any decor. *Example:* A forty-inch-tall, thirteen-inch-wide, maple ladder has three steps, each two inches wide. Hang it vertically so each of the steps can be used as a shelf, or horizontally so the sides become shelves.

Decorative wooden shelf

Select a color for each of your display shelves that highlights the particular treasures displayed on it. *Example:* Dark brown treasures do not show up well on black, brown, or some shades of green shelves. For a temporary change, you can cover a shelf with attractive paper or fabric. Paint shelves for a permanent change of color. Black shadowboxes make especially nice display units for white miniatures. Strings of miniature white Christmas tree lights are great for highlighting treasures displayed on shelves, especially cut-glass and silver miniatures.

To help insure against figurines and small vases vibrating and falling from woodwork casings or shelves, fold duct tape or packing tape in half to make double-sided tape and place on bottom of each treasure before placing it firmly on a shelf.

Other Display Units

Expandable wooden peg racks with ten pegs that expand to various lengths showing a large, open work, diamond background, are excellent for displaying such things as mugs, beer steins, baskets, and various other treasures. They aren't always available, so buy them when you can find them.

Hanging baskets ordinarily used for holding plants work nicely as display units for dolls, stuffed animals, bottles, and unique treasures. For dolls or stuffed animals that tend to slip, secure them with string, garbage bag twist-ties, paper clips, or safety pins. Conceal the fasteners under the sleeves or collars of clothing on the toy.

Wire coat hangers can be converted into similar hanging baskets for dolls and animals. Cover the entire surface of the hanger with fabric, yarn, wrapped ribbon, or decorative tape. Pull into a diamond shape. Set the treasure into the bottom point of the diamond and secure. The hook of the hanger can either be slipped over a curtain rod or door top, or hung on the wall.

Don't forget cupboard doors when you are decorating! Lightweight treasures or decorative pot holders can be taped onto wooden cupboard doors. Old-fashioned metal cupboards provide excellent decorating backgrounds: Just attach magnetic tape to the backs of treasures, or hang them on magnetic hooks.

A Few Display Suggestions

Don't shy away from trying unusual color combinations — you may be pleasantly surprised. If not, the display can easily be changed. *Example:* One rummager made a charming shelf display from a pink vase filled with lavender and pink artificial flowers. Country blue candles at the sides of the vase added pleasing accents.

Amber glass is an excellent, versatile decorating aid. It catches light well and is compatible with all backgrounds and nearly any texture, from fine china to pottery. Shades of green in different textures — from cut glass to glazed pottery — coordinate amazingly well. Silver adds a touch of elegance that can be used any time of the year with almost any decorating scheme.

Don't avoid unusual texture combinations. *Examples:* Milk glass with cut glass, smooth ceramics with unglazed pottery, cut glass with pottery. Such unthinkable put-togethers produce interesting and pleasing concepts. One pleasing combination I discovered is red ceramic heart flower planters with silver candle holders. Another unusual texture combination is a cluster of dried wheat in a transparent amber vase.

A display of cut glass creates a sparkling look during any season. It is especially nice during drab winter months. Good, bright light — either natural or artificial — enhances the appearance of cut-glass and brings out its sparkle. No home should be without at least one pair of nine-inch-tall cut glass bud vases. A combination of cut-glass and silver miniatures set into a black shadow-box and highlighted with white Christmas tree lights makes a striking display!

Pieces of wicker can be coordinated even when colors, blends, and textures vary. Wooden treasures of various types of wood — maple, oak, walnut, or cherry — can also be used together. Brass accents wood nicely as well.

Cut-glass vinegar bottle

Try Grouping Unusual Pieces

Don't hesitate to put strange collection pieces together. *Example:* For a person who collects fish, an interesting display can be created by using collection pieces that are unlikely partners — figurines, flower planters, salt and pepper shakers, a sugar bowl and cream pitcher, and a bottle opener with a fish head.

When shopping in secondhand marketplaces, you'll find that some treasures that seem too gaudy for your decor often take on a new appearance once you get them into your home surroundings. It is not unusual to find treasures that, at first glance, seem ugly because of shape, color, texture, or some other feature, but, later, reveal a degree of character in their "ugliness" that makes them interesting, appealing, and very useful.

Functional can be decorative. *Example:* An assortment of useful items assembled on the bottom shelf of a kitchen end table — including an emerald green cut-glass, fishbowl-shaped flower vase used as a catch-all and to support a ball of string the size of a volleyball; a sturdy, safe, amber candleholder with an ugly candle ready for any power outage emergency; a black Royal Haeger deer-shaped flower planter used as a container for boxes of wooden matches; and a manicure set — make an attractive display. The items are kept handy in a decorative way.

Be daring! *Example:* A rummager found a collectible Spider Man light-switch plate in a grab bag box. The question was whether to save it or use it. He decided to install it in the bathroom, where it became a good conversation piece.

Displaying Decorator Tins

It's frequently difficult to display popular decorative collector's tins so their qualities are fully appreciated. This is especially true of round tins that need to be set on edge and of tins with attractive lid tops. To set round tins and lids on edge for display on cupboard tops or windowsills, push them into a bed of modeling clay to hold in place. Double-sided tape is not recommended for this purpose because the tape might mar the finish of the tin.

You might also consider hanging tins for display to add a dimensional effect to a wall display. Remove the lid and make a loop of heavy string long enough to encircle the tin lengthwise plus an extra two inches. Lie the string loop on a flat surface, set the tin inside the loop, one inch from its top, and tightly stretch the string across the open top of the tin. Replace the lid to clamp the string in place. Pull the extra string at the end of the loop through the string at the back side of the tin to make a hanging loop. To help keep string from slipping, secure it with Scotch tape in the least obvious sections.

Another way to hang smaller tins is to replace the string with a heavy duty rubber band and run a paper clip or bread twist-tie through the hanging loop to make it more stationary. Hanging tins with rubber bands is preferable whenever possible because they are easier to work with, and they stay in place without being secured with tape. Sometimes it's best to store the bottoms of the tins and to hang only the lids, using the wire and spring hangers made for decorator plates. A wall grouping of tins and lids enhances and emphasizes the dimensional look.

Many large metal serving trays have appealing pictures suitable for hanging. Wire and spring plate hangers can be stretched to accommodate these trays as well.

Treasure Hunter's Tips

RECYCLING OLD TREASURES

Finding new uses for old, discarded items is one of the great challenges — and sources of satisfaction — in rummaging. The possibilities are numerous. Here are just a few ideas to get your thinking started.

Old and new brooches can be found priced from a quarter to a dollar in secondhand marketplaces. Buy an assortment and pin them on the yoke of a lady's jean jacket to add a one-of-a-kind designer touch to your wardrobe.

Three-ring school notebooks used for holding loose-leaf paper make great albums for baseball cards.

One rummager was so delighted with the purchase of a satin ribbon holding five old metal bells that he didn't want to wait for Christmas to display the treasure, so he found a new use for the ribbon of bells — as a wind chime!

A wooden jewelry box shaped like an old-fashioned treasure chest makes an intriguing addition to a rummager's nautical "sunken-treasure" decorating theme. Open the lid; fill the chest with pearls, silver and gold chain, and some costume jewelry with bright stones; accent the scene by propping a skeleton-head-shaped earring in front of the chest; and scatter small sea shells around it.

The cabinets and lids for old treadle sewing machines are made of high-quality wood that sometimes has lovely etchings or carvings in it. Remove the machine and use the cabinet to hold record albums or magazines. It's easy to look down into the box and locate what you're looking for.

A Mrs. Butterworth syrup bottle takes on a new function when a white tapered candle with a small decorative candle ring slipped around it is set in the neck.

A marble collection displayed in a clear glass bottle with an interesting shape makes a sparkling, showy decoration.

Small decorative touches can sometimes revive an old object. For example, tie a piece of decorative lace or ribbon around the neck of a bud vase.

Old flannel makes exceptionally good dust cloths — you can often find old flannel shirts priced cheaply in secondhand marketplaces. Remove the buttons before cutting into rags and save to use as replacements for lost ones. Store buttons in a clear glass bottle or jar and display as a nostalgic decorating accent.

Metal kitchen utility carts with three shelves that were popular in the 1950s and 1960s make an ideal stand for a small, portable gas grill, and the bottom two shelves are convenient for stacking barbecue accessories and dishes. These can sometimes be found for a dollar or less at garage sales.

A sturdy leather carrying case designed for an old-model Polaroid camera makes a great storage container for cassette tapes.

Some decorative one- to two-gallon plastic ice buckets are equipped with lids and handles. They make a great mini ice chest for a quart container of food being taken to a picnic.

Transform strips of lace into doilies. These work extra well on rectangular or hard-to-fit shelves. Lace can frequently be found on sale for fantastically low prices in fabric departments. It can also sometimes be found by the yard at garage sales. Or, buy old curtains with lace edgings at garage sales, remove the lace to make doilies, and cut the old curtains into useful rags. Two bargains for the price of one!

Dishes and accessories are usually plentiful and inexpensive in secondhand marketplaces. An unmatched assortment of dishes sparks up ordinary, everyday meals at home. Guests are intrigued by the variety in place settings — much more of a conversation piece than the standard set of matched china! But, remember that gold trim on old cups and plates is real gold — it cannot be used in a microwave oven.

You may find old cotton or cotton-blend tablecloths with floral designs in bright colors in excellent condition for nominal prices. If you haven't already tried them to add a touch of something different to your at-home dining, do so.

Many decorative sets of ceramic measuring cups that come in pleasing colors or have attractive designs are great for serving small amounts of sugar and cream for dinner guests.

Old sugar bowls and cream pitchers make unusual serving dishes for such things as cherry tomatoes, relishes, pickles, and dressings. Fancy old coffee cups also work well. A collection of sugar bowls and cream pitchers makes an interesting display on kitchen shelves or windowsills.

Beer goblets in a variety of colors and with numerous logos take on second lives as candy dishes, relish bowls, flowerpots, and vases for fresh flower arrangements.

Use a musical mug to make a fun candy dish. Guests, especially children, love being handed a mug full of candy playing music.

Mini Santa Claus head mugs are ideal nut cups. They also can be used for individual servings of cream and sugar. Or, hang the mini mugs on a Christmas tree as special decorations. The larger Santa mugs are natural dishes for candy canes and peppermints.

 Antique coffee cups with matching saucers, sugar bowls, and cream pitchers filled with small decorative soaps are often sold in gift shops and antique stores. Make your own versions for a fraction of the store-bought cost!

Coffee mugs, especially those that look like tree trunks, are excellent flowerpots for small plants. So are sugar bowls, cream pitchers, and teapots. This is a fantastic way to use lovely treasures that have small chips inside or broken lids. Small saucers or bowls, found economically priced in secondhand marketplaces,

work perfectly under flowerpots. Some rummagers buy chipped antique saucers just for this purpose. Large-size glasses with soda or beer logos can also be used as flowerpots or vases.

Use fruit jars, especially blue ones, to add accent to a country kitchen. One rummager advises me that the pint-size fruit jars are excellent containers for freezing peppers and onions.

The tiny eggcups for serving boiled eggs have multiple purposes: To hold decorated Easter eggs, as nut and mint dishes, as a gift container for a small treasure, or as a small remembrance gift when filled with candy.

Some clear-glass ashtrays have lovely patterns and sparkling finishes. Consider using them as soap dishes, candy dishes, or relish trays.

Wine and whiskey bottles in an assortment of sizes, shapes, and colors make good substitute vases. *Example:* A clear-glass wine bottle decorated with a frosted design of grape leaves and clusters became the perfect vase for a bouquet of roses when other vases were the wrong color or had openings that were too small. Every household should have at least one large milk-glass-bottle vase!

Don't overlook decorative Jim Beam whiskey bottles when you can find them. Decorated with everything from pictures of wildlife to those of famous artists and musicians, these bottles have many excellent qualities. Some are in fancy shapes; some pay tribute to civic and military organizations as well as special events. Many of the bottles have a biography of the artist who designed the picture and information about it on the back. They are fun to collect. Once a beginning interest is spawned, it grows quickly. And the bottles are adaptable to all decors, displayed as a collection unit or as individual accent pieces here and there.

For a different look in kitchen curtains (especially on short double windows) collect several old-fashioned good-quality cotton printed half-aprons that tie around the waist — depending on the fullness desired, four to six aprons are usually enough for one window. The aprons can be sewn together or tied by the apron strings around the curtain rods to form curtains.

Small metal recipe boxes from yesteryear are great catch-all boxes to clean up desk clutter. They are also excellent for storing current sales receipts of items with limited guarantees or for merchandise that might need to be returned.

Napkin holders, especially fancy wooden ones, make great letter holders. Ceramic household containers that originally held wooden kitchen utensils, flower planters, mugs, steins, and short vases all work as pencil holders. Just place a wadded-up paper towel in the bottom to catch ink drips. Glass dome-shaped "frogs" with holes used in floral arrangements are also the perfect size to convert into pencil holders. Cover the bottom of the frog with felt to protect table and desktops from ink marks made by uncapped ball-point pens.

A college student rummager found an appealing use for what many consider to be a "pain in the neck basket" — the over-sized oval basket with a hump in the bottom and a large handle seen in old-fashioned pictures of women gathering flowers. The rummager declared this type of basket to be an ideal magazine rack.

Use a flower planter shaped like a baby bassinet as a doll bed: Make a small pillow/mattress to fit the bottom of the planter, add a tiny doll, and cover with a made-to-order mini-baby blanket.

A large broken mirror can be cut into pieces and placed in small picture frames to create a collection of mini-mirrors. Use the mirrors alone in a wall display, or individual ones here and there to accent other treasure displays.

Wooden coffee table tops, scraps, and sections of old stereo or TV cabinets can all be made into cabinets or shelves. It is amazing what can be done with a few scraps of wood and some paint or varnish. I constructed a set of display shelves from scraps of ¼-inch-thick plywood, and then spray painted them. The shelves fit perfectly into the space allotted and were compatible with the existing woodwork. Moreover, they looked like quality wood.

Large stereo units constructed of quality wood popular in the 1960s and 1970s are now being given away or sold for incredibly low prices at secondhand marketplaces. They can be taken apart and salvaged for the wood, speakers, and various stereo components.

Old console TV cabinets also yield good quantities of quality wood, or they can be converted into wonderful display units. Simply remove the television unit and use as is, or mount shelves in the cabinet cavity.

Wrought iron TV tables and record stands can quickly be made into temporary end tables or display units. Cut a piece of heavy cardboard to fit any shelves on the unit. Spray paint the cardboard or cover it with a piece of colored poster board. Or, conceal it by covering with a doily, lunch cloth, or decorative towel. For a more elaborate and "finished" appearance, cover the shelves with pieces of wood.

TRY A NEW LOCATION FOR GIVING A TREASURE NEW LIFE

Treasures can be used in any location. Use children's wall plaques throughout the home to add a relaxed feeling and a touch of freshness. Hang clown wall plaques in the bathroom or a hallway, or to add a touch of charm to a living room. Use large pictures of Raggedy Ann and Andy gardening in almost any decor to add a look of spring. Hang a set of three metal wall plaques of baseball players on an opposite wall from the gardening pictures to tie the room together. Nursery theme cutouts do wonders for drab areas. For example, hang pressed wood cutouts of the cow jumping over the moon in a dreary hallway.

Wooden spice racks can be converted to whatnot shelves. Those that are approximately twelve inches square with two shelves and two small drawers work especially well. Remove any slats across the front. The drawers can either be left in for a decorative touch or removed so the space can house mini-figurines. Another attractive feature is that most of these racks are made of quality wood that needs nothing done to it.

SET THE SCENE FOR THE SEASON OR HOLIDAY

Half the fun of having so many treasures on hand is using them to create all kinds of new decorating schemes. You have the flexibility to easily change your surroundings to fit the season or a favorite holiday.

For fall, brown whiskey bottles make exceptionally nice vases for bouquets of either real or artificial daisies, cattails, or pussy willows. The bottles catch light well, so they are most effective placed where light can shine on and through them. A sprig of red oak leaves and a bouquet of white artificial flowers placed in an earthen or black vase is also fantastic.

Decorate a Tree

One fun and easy way to use your treasures for holiday celebrations is to keep a small (two- to three-foot) "Christmas" tree set up year-round that you can decorate according to the season or special holiday. I like a white flocked one but a green one is fine.

Decorating the tree with Valentine and Easter decorations is a fun way to chase away the "winter blahs." Following are a few seasonal decorating ideas.

Valentine's Day. Cut out paper hearts from red and pink construction paper or neon paper in shades of pink, lavender, blue and rose, trace around a wooden heart and fasten them to the tree. Children's valentines can also be added. Or, buy red heart-shaped lollipops and push their sticks amongst the boughs.

Easter. Use wires from Christmas decorations to hang colorful plastic eggs on the tree. Or, decorate the tree with two-inch-tall stuffed rabbits with hanging loops. Of course, the tree can also be decorated with commercial wooden eggs and ornaments. Try painting them yourself.

Fill a wicker basket with "Easter grass," add a stuffed or ceramic hen and set next to the tree. The effect is even better if tiny chicks or eggs are added. Mini-baskets filled with "grass" and tiny rabbits could also be hung on the tree.

April Showers. Visit the party department in a discount wholesale house and buy paper umbrellas used in mixed drinks. Stick them into the branches of the tree. Or, hang miniature plastic watering cans from the tips of the boughs.

Memorial Day. Decorate the tree with poppies or mini-flags.

Summer. Find pieces of jewelry or small toys shaped like pieces of watermelon, hot dogs, sunglasses, and other fun activities to decorate the tree.

Fourth of July. Stick mini-flags into the limbs.

Halloween. Decorate the tree with small plastic or stuffed owls, witches, ghosts, skeletons, and bats. Or cut figures from paper.

Thanksgiving. Using the same texture of treasures as for Halloween, decorate the tree with mini-Pilgrims, Indians, and turkeys, or miniature fruits, vegetables, and Indian corn.

Create Your Own Tree

The tree decorating idea is one of my personal favorites. We've had so much fun and have become totally engrossed in the pastime of searching for treasures to add to the scene. We've even taken it a step further and created our own tree.

We took a section of dead tree limb, approximately four feet tall and three feet wide at its widest point, with most of its natural bark still on. It has three nicely shaped branches with twigs extending from them. We fastened the "tree" into a metal Christmas tree stand and set it on top of the refrigerator with grass-green and chocolate-brown doilies draped around the stand to give it an earthen appearance. Ever since setting it up we've been decorating.

We created a swing by drilling a hole in each end of a one-half-inch-thick piece of plywood and cutting apart a hanging basket made of twine to use strands as ropes, which were knotted through the holes in the plywood. The swing is suspended from the lower branch on the limb. An eight-inch-tall pair of Raggedy Ann and Andy dolls sit on the swing seat. Double tape (made from packing tape) on their bottoms keeps them from sliding off the seat and garbage bag twist ties attach their arms to the ropes to look as if they are grasping them. A cardinal and three bold butterflies are clipped onto the twigs.

One and two at a time, more decorations have been added to the tree — including three sizes of birds with orange, yellow, brown, and white coloring; a pair of white doves; a pair of blue jays; a mini-bird nest with a blue bird and eggs in it; a Christmas decoration made from a walnut; another decoration shaped like a squirrel; a pair of tiny squirrels on a pick designed to stick in a flowerpot; an owl that probably originated in a McDonald's Happy

Meal; and a small turtle figurine, set to look as if it's crawling up the base of the tree "trunk."

Creating a ground scene beneath and around the tree was the next natural step. Again, treasures have been added one at a time as they were acquired — a white Scottish terrier figurine from the forties; a pair of frog-shaped salt and pepper shakers; a wooden wishing well; a lime green worm set on the end of a salt shaker that looks like a log; a small figurine of a deer; an authentic-looking outhouse; a snail made of rocks; a pair of skunk salt and pepper shakers; a small turtle bank; and an old-fashioned-looking wooden mailbox mounted on a base covered with pebbles and wildflowers.

This pet project is a constant source of pleasure. While we have tentative plans for decorating the tree for Halloween and Christmas, the final outcome will be more spontaneous than planned — as the ideas hit us and the treasures show up!

Using Figurines

Try setting up your own scene using the treasures you have. Actual figurines are difficult to find, and they are usually quite expensive when they are available. But many treasures are excellent substitutes for figurines. One obvious choice is small vases or mini-pitchers, especially those with delicate, molded flower decorations. Attractive collector's bells can also substitute for figurines. Or try toothpick holders shaped like figures and animals, ceramic and blown-glass pin cushions shaped like animals and figures, and character candles, banks, and salt and pepper shakers. Salt and pepper shakers are especially nice as figurine substitutes because of the large variety of designs and compatible sizes they come in.

Baseball bank

The most unusual and appealing bell-shaped votive candle holders (without candles) can also be turned upside down to use as "bells" in a decorating display.

Be creative as you think of places and ways to set up small scenes and displays around your home. Make houseplants more interesting by setting tiny figurines of frogs, turtles, squirrels, and other animals in the pots. It is also fun to set larger figurines or stuffed animals between and amongst the pots. For example, a one-foot-tall stuffed frog with a silly expression is a surprise decorating accessory which rouses chuckles of delight in almost any visitor discovering the frog for the first time.

I found a small mustard container shaped like a fire hydrant. It seemed appropriate to use the bright red ceramic container as the focal point for a display with three bone china dogs set around the hydrant. It was especially fitting that one of the tiny dogs was a Dalmatian.

WORDS OF ADVICE ON FIGURINES

Some tall, open vases or figurines (such as shoes) are top-heavy and tip over easily. Place a sufficient quantity of sand or small rocks in the bottoms of these to keep them upright. Use wooden and ceramic candle pedestals as display stands for figurines, dolls, stuffed animals, or small collectibles. The large solitary pedestal for a pillar candle and a stand with three to five separate "candle holders" for votive candles work equally well.

If you happen to have one of those figurines of a little boy fishing, don't just have it sit there looking cute. Put it to work in a scene to make it look as if the boy is actually fishing. Use an aqua-colored candy dish or a shallow, colored dish to create the illusion of a pond. Place small toy fish, fish figurines, or fish figurine substitutes in the pond. Then, set the boy on the "bank" with his fishing line dangling in the water.

Fill a medium-size fishbowl with water. Add artificial floating fish and aquarium accessories, and set a figurine of a cat so it looks as if it is peering into the fishbowl. Or, secure a stuffed cat on top of the bowl so it looks like it is ready to go fishing. Have fun!

CHRISTMAS DECORATING IDEAS

Christmas creates some special opportunities for rummagers to buy and use holiday treasures. Here are a few ideas.

Don't forget the bathroom when decorating! Who says that a giant Christmas stocking can't be hung on the bathroom wall or that a holly garland can't be draped over the top of the medicine chest? Use your imagination to decorate your bathroom — just as you would do any other room of the house. Every bathroom has room for at least one holiday figurine.

Use magnetic hooks to hang decorative holiday pot holders on refrigerators and metal cupboard doors. The decorations can also be taped on refrigerators or wooden cabinet doors.

Holly sprigs are great little decorations that can be taped almost anyplace — on cupboard doors, refrigerators, walls, windows, and mirrors.

Collect miscellaneous pieces of Tom and Jerry sets to make a decorative display. Add an aged nutmeg grater for a neat, old-fashioned look.

Christmas tree ornaments shaped like animals or people are excellent substitute figurines in displays. Small dolls, stuffed animals, or novelty items such as the California Raisins riding in a sleigh add a new touch to holiday decorating.

Go with surprises. Decorating ideas frequently come about by accident. For example, one rummager came home from a winter garage sale with a lovely large basket and set it in the middle of the table while unpacking other items. When some bouquets of just-purchased red poinsettias were thrown into the basket until there was time to put them away, the idea of a lovely Christmas centerpiece was created.

Red felt mini-bows taped to the sides or handles of baskets add a spark of seasonal cheer.

Spark up dull hallways or dark corners with decorations such as hanging baskets filled with Christmas flowers, garlands draped across doorways, candle ring wreaths, felt stockings, cutouts, or whatever small decorations strike your fancy and can be hung on the walls.

Place a hurricane lamp shade (preferably red) or a stuffed animal in the center of a candle ring to create an unusual centerpiece. Some small candle rings make exceptionally nice wreaths. They are light enough in weight to hang on cupboard doors as well as walls. For some uses, the ring's center hole may be too large or need something extra. To solve this problem just fill the center hole with a round Christmas tree ball, a Christmas tree decoration shaped like an animal, a small Santa Claus figure, a tiny doll, or a stuffed animal.

Remember that artificial Christmas trees of all sizes and descriptions can be found priced from $1 to $10 in secondhand marketplaces. Buy as many as you have room to store! Use some as is. Disassemble others to create smaller trees or centerpieces. If possible, set up several trees and decorate each with a different color, theme, or style of decorations. For example, decorate one tree with antique ornaments; one with only wooden ornaments; one with only handmade cloth decorations; and another with only blue balls.

To coordinate colors or create a tree topper for a small tree, remove the cap from a round Christmas tree ball. Place the ball upside down and insert the top sprig of the tree into the hole of the ball.

If you have the perfect location for an outside Christmas tree, but there is no live tree growing there, use an artificial tree instead. Decorate it with outdoor lights and weatherproof decorations. Or, decorate the tree with edible decorations for birds and squirrels.

The rummager who is lucky enough to have an old-fashioned metal basket once popular for holding funeral and wedding bouquets has a versatile decorating accessory. Paint the basket white and set a large, single, red poinsettia bloom in the basket. Place it in a solitary outdoor location. The basket is equally attractive filled with real or artificial seasonal flowers at other times of the year.

Flowerpots are inexpensively priced at summer garage sales, so buy them when available. Fill with poinsettias, pine boughs, or other plants for either indoor or outdoor Christmas decorating.

CREATE A SETTING FOR DOLLS AND TOYS

Dolls, stuffed animals, and toys are valuable decorating accessories — with the added bonus that many toys are collectibles with "book value" as well.

A doll's entire appearance and personality can be altered simply by changing its clothing. *Examples:* A baby doll can be turned into a little girl, a girl into a boy, or visa versa. One experienced fellow rummager witnessing such a change commented, "It used to be just a run-of-the-mill, average little girl. Now, it's an adorable little boy."

Dolls, bears, and rabbits are good showcases for antique baby clothing. Dress an old collectible doll in antique clothing and display it in an old high chair, buggy, baby bed, or bassinet.

Some dolls and toys can be used as substitute pieces of sculpture. Many stuffed animals are extremely realistic and add an unusual, natural appearance to home decor. *Examples:* Try setting a realistic white rabbit on the floor beneath a coffee table, a raccoon in a window, a squirrel on the back of an easy chair.

Add and enjoy sentimental touches by using childhood leftovers for decorating purposes. *Example:* A son's red Boy Scout beret on a large stuffed white St. Bernard creates an adorable effect as well as being a nostalgic reminder. One rummager dressed a little brown bear in one of her own baby dresses and placed her child's tiny infant gold ring on a pink satin ribbon and tied it around the bear's neck.

Use pieces of old costume jewelry as accessories for dolls and animals. Choose small earring and necklace fobs. String pieces of ribbon cut to fit through the loops on the tops of the jewelry pieces to convert them into tiny necklaces and bracelets.

Give Your Doll Something to "Do"

Dolls and animals are more interesting and seem to have more character when they are doing something. Put them into scenes where they are doing things such as playing cards, playing chess, having a tea party, reading a book, riding a toy, or simply holding

Treasures Add to Holiday Parties

Rummaging can make a major contribution to holiday parties — adding interest for guests and decreasing costs to hosts and hostesses. Keep ample quantities of candle holders on hand for party lighting effects, and treasures to use as gifts and door prizes. Secondhand baskets, trays, and tins are perfect for serving chips, pretzels, popcorn balls, and sandwiches at a buffet. A galvanized laundry tub filled with ice will keep canned and bottled beverages cold well into the morning after the party. It's also perfect to use when bobbing for apples!

Buy Halloween masks when you find them in secondhand marketplaces; they make a great addition to a party. Examples: If you're the host and hostess, pose for photographs wearing masks and convert the photos into homemade party invitations. Put masks on stuffed bears for unique decorating accessories, use as wall decorations, or stuff a pliable, full-head mask with newspapers or plastic bags and place it in a startling location (such as on the edge of the bathtub) for an eerie effect.

Use treasures to make fun, old-fashioned party games. Example: Fill a square, clear glass decanter (flour canister size) with water. Place a small votive candle holder or a toothpick holder of equal size in the center of the bottom of the decanter. With arm stretched at full length and hand over top of decanter, have guests drop pennies, one at a time, into the container. The first participant whose penny falls into the toothpick holder wins a prize — an appropriate treasure, of course!

Arrange various treasures such as glasses, mugs, flower planters, and ashtrays in a triangular formation on the floor to create an old-fashioned coin toss game. Supply guests with equal amounts of pennies. If a guest is lucky enough to have a coin land in a treasure, it's his. Be inventive! Use your imagination to create other games.

Clown figurine

a toy. Party favors and cake decorations can be used as accessories for the activities of dolls and animals.

One clown collector bought a toy plastic table measuring seven inches by ten inches by five inches tall at a toy department clearance sale. He cut a piece of scrap plywood to convert the table to plain top. For a nominal fee at a thrift store he bought three handcrafted chairs that were a perfect fit for the table, and set a trio of clowns in the chairs. Using miniature cards, he dealt each a poker hand. After a few weeks, he changed the scene. He covered the table with a red bandanna handkerchief, set up a magnetic travel chess board for two of the clowns, and set a miniature whiskey bottle in front of the third.

He then set a pair of more delicate lady clowns on display stands that could be adjusted so it appeared they were sitting on chairs. He made a table for them from a cardboard circle set on a short wrought iron candle holder covered with a circle of neon paper that coordinated with the colors in the clowns' clothing. The display was finished off with a crocheted doily made into a tablecloth and a miniature tea set on the table.

Don't limit your selection or use of toys: all ages and types of toys have their own appeal and fascination. Almost any toy can spark up your decor and become an interesting conversation piece. Most people are intrigued with remote control cars. Replicas of older models serve as nostalgic accents. Fisher-Price toys, especially the older wooden ones, are appreciated more by parents than by children.

Tops, particularly the old metal ones, are fascinating for both youngsters and oldsters, but difficult to find. Many youngsters have never played with one, possibly because the tops do not work their best on carpeted floors. And, the once popular toy jolts fond memories in older folks.

DECORATING WITH DOLLS

Set a cute doll in an attractive wicker basket and give the doll some toys of her own — perhaps a small Raggedy Ann doll or a tiny bear.

Use a desktop wooden bookcase, the type resembling a church pew or park bench as a seat for one or two dolls, or a collection of small stuffed animals.

Set an old doll for a ride on a toy wooden horse to add rustic charm.

Convert the decorative miniature picnic tables used to hold catsup and mustard dispensers into tables for small dolls or animals. Cover the table top with a piece of cardboard and make a tablecloth from a red bandanna or a piece of red checkered cloth.

Convert a smoking stand designed to hold a canister or tobacco and pipes into a miniature doll table and use a doily as a tablecloth.

Fill the bottom of an old-fashioned, brass flowerpot with cotton batting, set a small animal or doll in the pot, and hang it from a brass wall bracket for a plant.

Give a scholarly-looking bear a book to read.

Suspend dolls or animals with hanging loops from the curlicue loops on the bottoms of wrought iron sconces.

Set a large-size monkey in a hanging basket. Slip a rubber band over one wrist and stick the stem of a bunch of artificial bananas under the rubber band so it appears the monkey's holding them.

Wicker baskets are good display units for dolls and animals set on the floor. One rummaging couple I know set a pair of panda bears in baskets of an existing wall display. The result was a real attention getter — delighting visitors and fellow rummagers.

Display animals on the tops of doors that remain open all of the time. A Smurf doll set on top of an open kitchen door is unique, and classified, especially by children, as "neat."

Hang a brightly colored stuffed toucan in a kitchen or porch archway for a fun and different decoration that both home owners and guests will enjoy.

You've heard the expression "more fun than a barrel of monkeys" — fill a small barrel with stuffed monkeys and set on display.

To make a mini baseball glove for a doll, slit the bottom of an infant's squeeze toy so it will fit over the hand of the doll.

Before placing the "glove" on the doll, spray paint it brown or black, and make a baseball from a small styrofoam ball. Use a black marker to draw authentic-looking lines on the ball.

A large white rabbit dressed in children's bib overalls and a red bandanna handkerchief tied around its neck adds to a country kitchen look.

Fill a small laundry basket with toys. Keep it in an out-of-the-way but easily accessible location to have on hand when little friends visit.

PART THREE:

Selling Your Treasures

Everyone lives by selling something.

—Robert Louis Stevenson

Everything is worth what its purchaser will pay for it.

—Publilius Syrus (circa 42 B.C.)

CHAPTER 6

HOLDING YOUR OWN GARAGE SALE

Tastes change! Secondhand bargains afford rummagers the luxury of changing decorating accessories and schemes as frequently as you like. But sooner or later you're going to find it's time to part with some treasures to make room for others. The rummager who swears she will keep forever every single treasure bought will most likely end up having a garage sale eventually.

The best time to begin preparing for a garage sale is when you realize you have become an avid rummager who regularly buys secondhand treasures.

Keep records. As discussed on pages 6–9, mark your treasures with a price code system so you know at a glance how much you paid for the item. It is not advisable to leave original price tags on treasures, since when you have your own sale, those tags will have to be removed if you intend to turn a profit — a task that is too time-consuming to do when you're preparing for a sale. Besides, if one of the original prices goes unnoticed and is not removed, it can cause justified irritation in a potential buyer.

It is also a good idea to record the purchase dates of treasures. Even though the date doesn't necessarily reflect the exact era when the item was made, it can be important at a future date. Keep track of the date you bought new treasures as well. People have a tendency to forget exactly when even the most-loved treasures were obtained. Knowing the exact purchase date can increase their value when sold.

If small toys, beverage glasses, and other memorabilia from fast-food restaurants don't have the date or the name of the establishment printed on them, note the information on an adhesive label and affix it to the object. Many of these treasures are collectible almost instantly.

BUYING TO SELL

Some rummagers buy with the intention of reselling their second-hand bargains. This can be profitable, but there are also pitfalls. It is not advisable to buy items with the idea of reselling them at a time far in the future, say twenty years from now since trends change too quickly. What's collectible today may not be so then. My advice is: Buy now as cheaply as you can and sell quickly. A longtime flea market vendor put it more aptly, "Don't buy anything for longevity because trends change. What is here today is gone tomorrow." *Example:* A solid white, quality china platter with the name of the company and the date stamped on the bottom is now fifty years old. When it was purchased ten years ago, everybody said it was a really good buy that would appreciate with time. Today, none of the local antiques or flea market dealers want the platter because their customers are buying flowered dishes.

Never buy a treasure unless you really like it yourself. Don't buy an item you don't like just because you know it has a book value which far exceeds the purchase price. Don't buy an object because you think it might be old or because you know it is collectible. There is no guarantee that you can resell it for what you think it's worth or for a price you are willing to accept.

Fellow rummagers are searching for bargains; dealers are looking for even better bargain prices. They aren't going to pay you what they expect to get in a resale price. Even collectors are looking for bargains. It might take a long time to find a buyer for items you have for sale. It's no fun to be stuck with objects you don't really like. And, when you pass up a 25¢ item at a garage sale because you don't like it, don't kick yourself later if you see an identical item priced at $4 in an antiques shop. There is no guarantee that you would have been able to sell it at all, let alone for that price.

Just because items are priced high at antiques fairs, it doesn't mean your identical ones at home are worth an equal amount. *Example:* A Jim Beam whiskey bottle bought for a dime has a book value of $12.50. In reality, any item is only worth what a buyer is willing to pay. In this instance, if the buyer will pay only $1, then that is all the bottle is worth.

KEEP TRACK OF WHEN YOU BOUGHT IT

You never know when you might want to sell a treasure you've bought — and one of the first things a potential buyer is going to ask is how old the object is. Even if you don't know the exact age of the item, knowing when you bought it is a good beginning.

For example, at a garage sale, you buy a bank which appears to be old, but there is no way to determine its exact vintage. Record the purchase date in an inconspicuous place on the treasure. If you decide to sell the object ten years later, you can at least tell the buyer how long you have owned it, which might help him or her determine the exact age of the treasure.

Buy as cheaply as you can when you intend to resell the merchandise. You can't pay $4 for an item on the assumption that you will be able to sell it for $15. Being old enough to be classified as "antique" or "collectible" does not guarantee that an item is valuable or that it can be resold.

Picking a Date and Time

Every seller has his own idea of when the best time is to have a garage sale. From the beginning to the end of garage sale season, strategic street corners are littered with garage sale signs on Fridays and Saturdays. A surprisingly large number of rummagers prefer to shop during the week when crowds are smaller. And, many sellers would rather have their sales during the week as well. *Example:* Two post-retirement-age women have had their garage sales on Tuesdays and Wednesdays for several years. They explained, "We've been doing it this way for all of these years, and it works. We don't have a lot of room. There are too many people on Saturdays. They come in, and they leave without buying. When there's such a big crowd, people can't get around, and they can't see what we have for sale. And, there are so many sales on Saturdays, people don't take time to look. They just go in and out. When we have sales on these days, people buy!" Another garage sale hostess had a similar opinion, "People have too much to do on weekends. More come during the week."

Winter months are excellent sale times. Rummagers want to rummage all year long, and there are few locations for rummaging expeditions during winter months — especially in areas with adverse winter weather conditions. With the decreased number of garage sales, rummagers eagerly look forward to finding new secondhand marketplaces.

Setting Hours of Operation

How long a sale should last is another matter of varied preference. Some sellers have short sales — one-day sales or those that last only three to five hours. The latter seems too short to hardly be worth all the preparation that goes into a garage sale. Then, there are average, two-day-long sales, and longer sales which last four or five days. One veteran garage sale hostess has had an annual, two-day-long sale for several years. She now declares that any future sale will last only one day. She reports having good crowds on Fridays, but rummagers hesitate to come on Saturdays because they assume the treasures are too picked over.

One common complaint among garage sale hosts and hostesses is that rummagers arrive on the scene too early — sometimes hours before the sale is scheduled to begin. The sellers aren't ready for customers, and the buyers want to shop immediately. To help eliminate this problem, do as much as you can the night before the sale so you're all ready to start at your scheduled time. When possible, set up your display tables and lay out all of your merchandise ahead of time. Then, when it is time for your sale to begin, all you have to do is unlock and open the doors.

Don't stick to a scheduled closing time. If rummagers are present or approaching, keep your eye off your wristwatch!

CHOOSING A LOCATION

Garage sales can easily be held in basements or enclosed porches all year long. And, electric space heaters make nice garages comfortable enough to house garage sales during winter months.

Large empty buildings in some communities are used as locations for group garage sale/flea market settings. It might be well worth your time and expense to set up a booth in such a marketplace. Shoppers buy! This type of secondhand marketing has the potential of becoming a popular trend. Weekly flea markets are a great way for owners to utilize buildings that would otherwise be sitting idle. Building owners can make a few extra bucks; sellers can turn summer incomes into year-round pocket money. And, rummagers can continue searching for treasures.

A perfect situation would be to have a basement or porch where treasures can be displayed, store-fashion, and left in place for additional sales when time permits.

Unfortunately, not everyone wishing to have an at-home garage sale is blessed with a good environment. Many sellers do not have a nice garage, a roomy basement, or even a nice porch where they can display merchandise. This does not prohibit them from having garage sales. Do the best with what you have, even if it is a dark, shabby garage.

Use fans to cool garages in hot weather. Heat garages in chilly or cold weather. One garage sale hostess swore her customers stayed longer and bought more because her garage was heated.

Extremely hot or cold weather conditions tend to curb rummagers' enthusiasm. But, thunderstorms and snow do not stop them. *Example:* One seller was dismayed by the number of people who came to her garage sale during an intense thunderstorm. She proclaimed that she would never go to a garage sale in that kind of weather. Yet, she didn't cancel her sale. Another hostess reported that the most unusual request from a rummager came from an eighty-year-old man in the heart of a drenching thunderstorm. He was serious when he asked the woman if she had any umbrellas for sale. Still another seller/rummager confided, "I'll go to a garage sale in the middle of a blizzard as long as the roads are open so I can get there." Thus, consider having a "rain or shine" sale and advertise that it will not be canceled because of bad weather.

Good lighting is essential: people need to be able to see to get around, and they won't buy items they can't see! It is not easy to light some sale locations, particularly old garages without plug-ins or even electricity. Run extension cords if necessary, but use extreme caution! Do not use frayed or damaged cords that might cause electrical shocks or fires. Arrange cords so shoppers will not trip over them. It is extremely beneficial to light special display areas in dreary locations. For example, the sheen and high quality of cut glass and colored glassware are enhanced by lighting.

Don't be discouraged if you have small crowds. This is an advantage when garages are small or space is limited.

ADVERTISING

When you're holding a garage sale, advertise in any available source. Most communities have a shoppers' advertising guide that comes out once a week, plus a daily newspaper. Check around; sometimes rummagers prefer one source over another. When attending other people's garage sales, ask where they advertised.

Ask fellow rummagers or customers at your own sale where they saw the advertisement. This will help you know how to get the most for your advertising dollars at your next sale. *Example:* If thirty people say they saw your ad in the local newspaper while only three referred to the weekly shopper, it is practical to spend more for newspaper advertising and less for ads in the weekly shopper.

Before placing your newspaper ad, check to see if there are special garage sale rates. *Example:* As incredible as it might sound, one rummager saved $40 by placing a garage sale ad instead of a general classified ad.

Post handmade notices on bulletin boards in supermarkets and laundromats. Word-of-mouth advertising is some of the best there

GET OUT THE WORD

*O*ne of the most important parts of having a garage sale is getting the word out before and on the day of your sale. Find out what the most effective means of advertising are in your area. Here are a few suggestions:

- *Buy an ad in the weekly shoppers' guide.*
- *Buy an ad in the "garage sale/flea market" section of your local newspaper.*
- *Post handmade signs on bulletin boards in supermarkets, laundromats, libraries, restaurants, and other area businesses with bulletin boards.*
- *The day before the sale, post very visible signs around your neighborhood, with clear arrows pointing to your location.*
- *The day of your sale, mount a large, colorful sign with balloons or some other eye-catcher in front of your house. If your garage door is closed due to inclement weather, post a large "Welcome, Please Enter" sign so rummagers know the sale is on and they should come on in.*
- *If you have goods for sale on more than one level or area of your yard or house, post clear signs directing people to these spots.*

is. The added bonus is that it is free. However, be warned it can also be the worst advertising. Dissatisfied customers will warn fellow rummagers not to waste their time coming to your sale if it is below standards.

Help Rummagers Find Your Sale

Post signs! Don't lose sales to those who post signs when you haven't. Many rummagers arrive at sales by chance because of posted signs, but don't find advertised sales because there are no signs near their locations. You've wasted your advertising dollars if no one can find your sale.

Mount large, colorful, easy-to-read signs on wood or cardboard. Use colors that stand out — hot pink and lime green are especially good, but almost any bright color is adequate. Sales go unnoticed if the signs are too small or drab, too limp, or flapping in the wind, making it impossible to read from a distance.

Bouquets of balloons attached to signs are excellent attention-getters. They are also great guideposts to exact sale locations when they are attached to the garage, especially if it is located in an alley. The more difficult a sale is to find, the more signs you need!

If you are having a garage sale and the weather is bad so you are forced to close the large door, post signs pointing to the alternative entrance and advising rummagers to *Walk In*. If no such sign is posted, some people will drive on by assuming the sale's been canceled. They are hesitant to approach a house where the garage is closed and there is no sign of activity.

Would you try to find a sale that was advertised the following way and where there were no signs posted? "Garage Sale: One block from high school stadium." Where? In which direction? Remember, neighbors who are *not* having garage sales frequently have full garages that look like sales, especially if the home owners are working in them. Your sale could be passed by if no signs are posted.

Treasure Hunter's Tips

ATTRACTING BUYERS

Remember, most secondhand merchandise is bought because the buyer wants it, not because he needs it. The market and buyers will only tolerate so much when it comes to poor attitude and high prices. The quality of merchandise, the attitudes of sellers, a supply of unique treasures, and prices combine to draw or discourage crowds. Here are a few tips for attracting and keeping buyers.

Rummagers love bargains! Treasures are fun to buy when they are low priced and high quality.

Be friendly and polite to customers. Snooty is a turn off.

Be cheerful! Have a good time. It makes shopping fun for the buyers. They tend to stay longer and spend more. Besides, it makes time pass more quickly for the seller. If you don't intend to have a good time, don't bother having a sale. Laughing, joking, and making bargains in tones rummagers can hear arouses interest and draws crowds.

Be in control. As hard as it is to believe, there are shoplifters at garage sales. Watch for them, but don't hover so intently that you offend honest rummagers and chase them away. They know what you're doing, and they are insulted. When rowdy rummagers are rough with treasures, inform them the merchandise is breakable. You don't need that kind of customer. If they break your merchandise, you lose anyway, so it doesn't matter if they get mad and leave before damaging anything.

Be aware of trivial things that often turn rummagers off. It is annoying when a seller is talking on a cordless phone when customers are present. Do business now, chat later!

Encourage responsible children, even pre-teens, to help with your sale. Some youngsters are very competent and businesslike. Compliment them when they are doing a good job. They should be recognized and given credit for doing a great job. If they make a mistake, wait until you are in private to criticize. Don't do it in front of customers. If you have teenagers who want to put on their own garage sale, encourage them to do so. They also have treasures to dispose of, and a garage sale is a good way for them to earn extra pocket money.

Be prepared to feel a twinge of sadness when some treasures sell! Although it is sad to see them go, it is a good feeling to realize that you have such good taste that other people want what you have. On the flip side, sometimes you'll have really neat treasures for sale or items that have a published book value of dollars more than the price you have on them and they won't sell. It is disappointing when no one seems interested in such treasures. But often an item will sell at a later sale.

Rummagers are annoyed when sellers do not provide newspapers for wrapping delicate treasures. It is even more irritating when the seller has no sacks or boxes available for carrying treasures.

Be prepared for children. It is understandable that small people will be present at many sales. Parents, both buyers and sellers, should encourage their children to be courteous, to be cautious about not running into rummagers, and not to leave toys lying around for shoppers to trip over.

Don't make smart-aleck remarks that you assume your customers will take as being jokes. *Example:* One rummager asked a flea market vendor if she accepted checks. The lady responded, "Sure, if they're good." The offended gentleman snapped, "Of course it's good." He then strode away without making a purchase. A few minutes later, the man again walked past the vendor's tables. She called out to him. "I do take checks. I was just kidding." The rummager ignored her.

Impressions linger! Avid rummagers do not return to sales where the merchandise was dirty, the quality was poor, the prices were high, or the seller's attitude was bad.

Keep things clean. It is amazing how many people are annoyed by seeing dirty flower planters for sale. It is not safe to assume a rummager is buying a flowerpot or planter to put dirt in. There are numerous other uses for these objects. They should be clean when they are put out for sale.

Make your sale worthwhile. Don't put out a scant amount of merchandise. Do you really want to spend a minimum of one day tending a sale where there are only a few items to sell? Rummagers don't want to waste their time and gas going to garage sales where there is not a quantity of treasures to choose from.

Concentrate on having a variety of merchandise — something for everybody. Ordinary items are okay, but unique treasures are needed! Avid rummagers rely on rummaging when they need common, everyday items. But, for the most part, they want interesting, neat "stuff" — clothing, treasures, toys, dishes, furniture, other household odds and ends, unusual objects, and things for automobiles. You can never predict what rummagers will buy!

DON'T SAY IT WON'T SELL

*A*lmost everything can be sold. One incredible grouping of items for sale at a flea market was a collection of old, broken, metal toys. Buyers need parts when restoring. The parts can sometimes be found in what appears to be nothing but a box of junk.

Most rummagers are unpredictable and fickle. An item they aren't interested in today is exactly what they need tomorrow or next week. So, regardless of what it is, someone is going to want it for something sooner or later.

Some rummagers buy parts of treasures — teapots without lids, half of a pair of salt and pepper shakers, or the top or bottom of a hen on nest — because they already have the corresponding part or because they are willing to wait for it to show up.

While it is true that rummagers, and especially dealers, do not buy damaged merchandise, never is a misconception. This is particularly true when it comes to toys and figurines. Buyers frequently restore or repaint such items.

Don't put out anything that is not for sale! Rummagers will try to buy anything that is not nailed down. Toys children have been playing with, tires, pieces of lumber are all targets for rummagers with keen eyes.

Don't try to make a buck by selling items that you would normally throw away. Rummagers recognize get-rich-quick schemes. This discourages them from buying your quality items.

On the other hand, don't throw something away just because it looks too old! Valuable treasures are lost this way. *Example:* One lady who was having her first garage sale confided that she had found a half dozen old dolls in her deceased mother's home. She had thrown them away because they were so old she didn't think anyone would want them. What a loss!

Think twice about disposing of items that you might not be able to replace because they have become obsolete in the secondhand marketplaces. *Examples:* The amber glass, Christmas candle rings, collectible beverage glasses, and Jim Beam whiskey bottles that could be found in almost every secondhand marketplace two years ago but are now scarce.

Take good care of your treasures. It is disappointing when a really neat item has a piece missing. It is depressing when a valuable treasure has been treated like a piece of junk instead of having been treated with care. When a seller takes pride in merchandise, even though it is being sold, his attitude is contagious and items sell better.

Attracting Vendors as Buyers

Make it a point to know your local flea market vendors and antiques dealers. When having a major sellout sale or a moving sale, contact your dealers. Many of them welcome the opportunity, but they want first chance at your treasures. They want the "best stuff," not the leftovers.

The dealers might not pay prices as high as everyday rummagers because they are buying for resale, and they need a profit margin. But, most dealers are fair, and they are great to do business with.

Apply the attitude that you aren't going to get rich quick! Price your wares so that you can retrieve your original investment and, maybe, make a little profit. Yet, sell low enough that the dealer can also make a profit. *Example:* You buy an item for a quarter. You sell it for fifty cents to a flea market vendor who in turn sells it for a dollar. Everyone doubles his or her investment. However, don't be surprised or upset if you see your old treasures priced at three or four times the amount you received for them. Even if you accepted a lower amount from a dealer than what you were asking for a treasure, you made a positive sale. There is no guarantee you could have sold it to someone else at all, let alone for your asking price. And, the more people who handle your wares, the higher the risk of damage. That risk was eliminated when the dealer bought your merchandise. So, sometimes it is better to take a little less and make a positive sale.

One disadvantage of selling to flea market vendors is that they frequently put out so many of your old treasures that there is nothing new for you to buy. You'd be buying back your old treasures.

PREPARING AND DISPLAYING YOUR MERCHANDISE

Garage sales are energy- and time-consuming. Advance preparation pays off. Keep your treasures clean all of the time so you won't have to take time to clean when preparing for the sale.

Don't try to conceal flaws. Have them visible or indicate their existence on a tag placed on the object. Or, ask the buyer if he or she noticed the damage — crack, chip, or missing part. Even if the price is only a nickel, buyers expect quality. Some even expect perfection. It is most likely not their intention to buy faulty junk without knowing it.

Don't hesitate to move your merchandise around during the sale. If it is not selling, people might not be seeing it. Or, the treasures might not be catching light well enough to show their true beauty. *Example:* A couple lived in a region where blue cut glass is difficult to find in secondhand marketplaces. When pieces can be found, they are snatched up quickly. The couple had some quality pieces of blue glass for sale at a garage sale. Why they were not selling was a mystery until they moved the pieces from a rather dark corner to a display area where direct sunlight enhanced the quality of the glass. Then, the glassware sold instantly.

Be prepared to answer questions. Buyers frequently ask what items are, how old they are, and any number of other questions. They expect sellers to have the answers. Be prepared! Even though you might not know all of the answers, answer as many questions as you can.

Treasure Hunter's Tips

SETTING UP AND DISPLAYING YOUR TREASURES

Tape lids on containers — teapots, sugar bowls and beer steins — to help guard against breakage by rummagers.

Never stuff merchandise into boxes set on the ground or floor. This is even less advisable when the items in the boxes are breakable glass or ceramics at great risk of being damaged. Even more risky, a customer might be cut on broken glass.

Use old dish drainers for displaying plates, record albums, or picture frames.

Display jewelry to bring out its best potential and keep pieces from becoming tangled or lost. Make display boards from large pieces of cardboard, cover with white paper, and affix necklaces and earrings with straight pins. Brooches can be mounted with their own fasteners.

Hang sale clothes on clotheslines set in a strategic location.

One seller came up with this creative idea for displaying sale clothing at a basement sale: Rest a suspension ladder horizontally across basement ceiling braces, and place clothes hangers on the ladder's steps.

When selling a collection of door knobs, mount them on a piece of wood to show how they will look on a door.

Picnic tables with attached benches are poor display units. The benches restrict rummagers from reaching and closely examining items displayed on top of the table. And, merchandise displayed on the benches is frequently knocked off by shoppers reaching for objects on the table.

Don't display items by scattering them on the ground unless it is absolutely necessary! Many people don't like to bend over to shop — others can't bend over.

Avoid setting boxes of ordinary items in places where they block access to displays of quality treasures. Many rummagers won't waste time sidestepping the boxes. Utilize wall space for hanging pictures, mirrors, pinup lamps, and whatnot shelves.

SETTING PRICES

An expert I saw on TV echoed the sentiment of most avid rummagers and sellers of secondhand merchandise, "Supply and demand creates valuables. Treasures are only worth what someone is willing to pay."

Know the competitive market. Garage sale leftovers with $5 and $10 price tags on them commonly turn up at thrift stores. In many instances, the going rate charged for the same items by the thrift store is 50¢ or 75¢. Another example is garage sale hosts and hostesses trying to sell sweatshirts for $3 to $5 when they cost 75¢ at a popular local thrift store.

It's as simple as this: If prices are too high, the merchandise won't sell. If it is given to a thrift store, there is no profit at all. Reduce prices to make at least some profit.

There comes a point in a sale when the seller has to make a choice: reduce prices and sell the items, stand pat and try to sell the wares at another sale, keep and continue using the treasures, or give them to charity and make nothing. Whether you are having the sale to get rid of stuff or to make money is a major factor in making your decision. Another result of prices that are too high is damaged merchandise from too many people handling and not buying.

If rummagers or collectors want to pay antique prices, they will go to an antiques shop. Dealers won't pay a price they can't turn a profit on.

When it is a moving sale, the object is to dispose of items you either no longer want, don't have room for, or don't want to move. Rummagers expect to find lower prices at moving sales.

If you really want to sell items, it is sometimes necessary to lower prices. Many objects are bought because they are not only appealing, but because the price is right. When a sale is drawing to an end, it is better to sell at a reduced price than to make no sale at all.

Be Willing to Bargain

When a buyer offers you a lower amount for your merchandise, you don't have to accept the offer. But, don't turn down a hot prospect with the idea that he or she might return tomorrow when you are more willing to bargain. Chances are the buyer won't return; he or she is not going to waste time returning because you might still have the item and be willing to sell it for less.

Being willing to dicker and deal is a good business trait. When it comes to bargaining, whether you decide to reduce your prices or not, be decisive! Don't be hesitant and wishy-washy. A firm *yes* or *no* is what the buyer wants to hear!

Some sellers set prices higher than what they expect to get with the intention of bargaining. Some buyers never ask sellers to reduce prices. They simply decide they don't want to pay the amount, and they leave without buying anything.

If you are involved in a garage sale with other participants and you'll be absent from the location for a while, authorize someone to reduce your prices or bargain for you and tell them what prices are acceptable. Most rummagers who are offering lower prices will not pay your higher asking price simply because you're not there to negotiate with.

Someone should be on the scene at a sale at all times. It is surprising how many times sellers display their wares at garage sales or flea market booths and then disappear. People can't buy if there is no one to give the money to, and what about theft? *Example:* On one occasion, a large crowd of rummagers gathered at a flea market vendor's location. He was nowhere to be found. Everyone in the crowd grew irritated. When the man finally appeared, everyone left. No one bought a single thing.

It is common practice for items priced at a quarter or even higher that are not selling to be grouped in a "bargain box" where they sell for a price from 25¢ to $2. At least the seller is making something and disposing of unwanted merchandise without having to make a delivery trip to a thrift store.

Some sellers use old-fashioned adding machines to tally up sale amounts. This is a great idea if you have one. If there is any dispute about the total amount due, it is convenient to be able to refer to the printed data on the adding machine slip.

Price Tags

Price tags are important because many people are too shy to ask. Instead of asking, they just won't buy.

A color-code price system — using different colored price tags to represent different prices — has advantages and disadvantages. The actual dollar amounts are not written on the circles. Instead, large posters are displayed revealing the corresponding colors and amounts (red circles equal 25¢, yellow circles equal 50¢, blue circles equal 75¢, and a green circle equals $1). You'll need numerous posters in obvious locations. The advantage is that this method saves a lot of time for the seller. The disadvantage is that many shoppers have difficulty comprehending the system. For some reason, they are frustrated when the amounts aren't written on the labels. This is particularly true in areas where use of this type of system is new.

Price tags made from masking tape are really not desirable. They wrinkle, ink fades, pencil writing does not show up well. In general, they are too difficult to read. However, if you still insist on using masking tape, keep these factors in mind: Use large pieces of masking tape; keep them smooth; and use large dark lettering. White adhesive medical tape works better than masking tape, because it peels off easily, and does not leave a great deal of glue residue on treasures.

Some sellers use price tags made from slips of paper and attached with cellophane tape. *Example:* One garage sale hostess used peach-colored pieces of paper with red writing on them. They showed up amazingly well.

Price tags with strings attached are sometimes hung around the necks of figurines, looped through handles of various treasures, or taped onto objects.

Large price tags are best. Regardless of the style used, the writing should always be prominent. Make it as large and as dark as possible.

Placement of price tags is a problem. Some harm finishes when removed. Yet, prices need to be in easy-to-see locations. If they aren't obvious, some shoppers won't look for them. And, if the rummager has to pick a treasure up to find the price, the risk of damage is increased.

Some rummagers prefer to have price tags left on their purchases so they don't have to rely on their memories about how much items cost. This is particularly true of rummagers who are keeping records or who are buying for resale.

It is common practice for participants in multiple-party sales to remove price tags to keep track of how much money each participant has earned. A quicker and easier method of keeping track of who sold what is to keep a chart. Divide a piece of paper into columns, each headed with the name of a seller. Whenever a sale is made, record the price of the item in the column under the owner's name.

Some sellers price wares by taping price tags on tables in front of objects with corresponding prices. This is not a good method, especially with more than one price group. Objects get moved and frequently end up with another price group. Items need to be individually marked unless all objects are the same price.

Some sellers use price charts listing bulk prices. *Example:* All jeans, $1. Sweat shirts, 75¢. Blouses, 50¢.

WRAPPING

Wrapping paper and sacks are essential! Having an ample supply of wrapping paper, sacks, and boxes is a major part of a successful garage sale. Rummagers do not want to spend a lot of money for treasures that they then have to juggle and risk dropping or losing on the way to their cars. They expect to have them put into sacks or boxes.

Also, rummagers expect to have delicate breakables wrapped! They do not want to have their new-found treasures broken before they even get them home — especially if the breakage is caused by inadequate wrapping.

When you are planning a garage sale, concentrate on collecting materials that can be used for wrapping sale items. This is a great way to recycle materials you would otherwise throw away. Plus, it cuts expenses and impresses customers.

Newspaper is a long-time standard wrapping material. Old sewing patterns are excellent. They are soft and come in assorted sizes. Watch for treasures you buy at garage sales or thrift stores to be wrapped in pattern pieces. Then, save them for your own future needs.

Save used fabric dryer sheets for wrapping — the added pleasant bonus is a faint leftover fragrance in the sheets. Plastic grocery bags can also be used as wrapping, as long as you set aside enough for actually carrying the merchandise. Dry cleaner bags are good for large items. Or, they can be cut into a sizable quantity of small wrappers.

Don't overlook bread sacks, an unusual wrapping material. Shake the bread crumbs out, save the sacks, and store in empty paper towel roll tubes. The sacks can be easily pulled out, one at a time, as needed, and the tubes can be conveniently stored in a box or paper bag.

Groupings of small treasures such as Christmas tree decorations and tiny toys can be packaged in zip-seal, plastic bags — if the added expense of the bags is warranted by the treasures. This packaging keeps small items together and keeps them easily visible as well. Reduce expenses by purchasing the least expensive brands of zip-seal bags. Better yet, when you purchase treasures packaged this way, save the bags to reuse at your own sale.

Small paper sacks (lunch bag variety) make good wrappers for figurines, mugs, and water glasses. The bags make wrapping and unwrapping less time-consuming. They are inexpensive and can be recycled. Many sellers package golf balls in egg cartons, which also make good packaging for many other small items.

CHAPTER 7

OTHER WAYS OF SELLING

A one-shot garage sale or yard sale works well for people who clean house once or twice a year. But the avid rummager may need more frequent opportunities to sell goods. This requires a bit of commitment to keeping your goods organized in a way that makes them easy to set up and display as needed. Here are two options for expanding your sales opportunities.

SELLING BY APPOINTMENT ONLY

Here is a unique type of garage sale which might interest you: an indoor sale *by appointment only*. This is for the seller with a large quantity of treasures to sell who has limited space. While such a sale can be held in a garage, basement, or porch, it is designed for the seller who has no set-aside sale space. Appointment sales allow the host and/or hostess to conduct a sale within the confines of their home. This type of sale is not for everyone! It requires patience, and means having strangers wandering through your home. Some sellers consider this an invasion of privacy. It requires having your normal living environment disrupted and living with litter for days. Items do not sell as quickly as they do at regular garage sales because the flow of shoppers is restricted.

Your ad is important. Label it "Indoor Garage Sale By Appointment Only." Highlight your sale items as you would for any other garage sale ad, but list your telephone number instead of your address.

Using an answering machine can be both an advantage and a disadvantage. It is great for screening calls and taking messages when you are not at home or busy with a customer. However, it is best to answer your phone when you can. Many callers are intimidated by answering machines and will not leave a message under any circumstances. Besides, you save the expense of returning long-distance calls.

Most callers are considerate about what time they call, but some people aren't. They apparently think that because they are awake to make calls, you will be awake to receive them. You can expect to receive calls as early as five in the morning and as late as midnight.

The most difficult aspect of this type of sale is knowing how much time to allow for each appointment. Some rummagers will take only fifteen minutes to look over your wares while others will need an hour or longer to shop. A reasonably safe, average amount of time to allow for each appointment is one-half hour. If you schedule back-to-back appointments and the first shopper does not stay the entire thirty minutes, you have the luxury of a break between buyers. If your customer is a dealer buying for resale, you might need to allot several hours for the appointment.

Ask callers for their names and phone numbers so that you can reach them if a scheduling change has to be made. This is an especially good practice if the caller originally wanted an appointment time that was already filled. But don't press the issue; some callers are eager to give you the information while others don't want to do so.

If you are selling appliances, furniture, or unusual pieces, make a list of the items and their prices and post it in obvious locations of your home. Have extra copies to hand out to your shoppers.

They might study the list more closely in the privacy of their own homes. Or, they might pass the lists on to new prospects. Also, post copies of your list, including your phone number, on bulletin boards in supermarkets and laundromats.

Advantages of Selling By Appointment

When you sell by appointment, the flow of shoppers can be channeled so there aren't too many people in a small space at one time. Rummagers need to be able to move around and pick out items they want.

The problem of shoppers arriving before a sale is scheduled to begin and before you're ready is eliminated. Likewise, you are not confined to the sale location for hours or days at a time. Appointments allow leeway and luxury in scheduling your time.

Shopping is more convenient and pleasurable for your customers. Treasures can be arranged in displays on walls, shelves, and tables so prospective buyers can see how they look in place and what items coordinate with each other.

Appointments enable sellers to have specific items readily accessible for buyers. *Example:* If a lady calls and says she is interested only in teapots, the seller can gather all of the available teapots and place them in an attractive display on a table before the potential buyer arrives. Or, if a rummager declares that he is searching for Christmas decorations, it is much more convenient to fetch the boxes of ornaments from a hard-to-get-to closet before the shopper arrives. Limited space sometimes prohibits sellers from displaying all sale merchandise at one time.

Being surrounded by the sale items right in your home allows you to continue with unfinished pricing or reduce prices as time permits. It is also easier to see when some displays are getting lost or overlooked and need to be moved to more noticeable locations.

Silver teapot

Shoppers like the personal touch. Some have observed, "It is like having your own personal showing." That is exactly what a garage sale by appointment is. Rummagers have ample time to shop leisurely. They don't have to worry about banging into other rummagers or about having someone snatch a treasure right out from under them. If special help or attention is needed, or if the shopper has questions to ask, you are right there and able to offer undivided attention.

Drawbacks of Selling By Appointment

With the sale set up right in your home, it is often too disruptive to continue it on a long-term basis.

Some people are a little uncomfortable looking around for items in your home, and are afraid they will pick out things that aren't for sale. Assure them the pieces that are sitting around and hanging on the walls are for sale. Tell them up front if certain areas or items are off-limits and guide their attention to specific sale areas.

Some people who have never seen a garage sale advertised "by appointment" have trouble understanding the concept. They ask, "Why do I have to have an appointment? Why don't you just tell me your address and let me come whenever I want to come?" Explain the circumstances! The limited amount of space cannot accommodate forty people at once. The format is for the benefit and comfort of the customer and enables the seller to have special items ready for the potential buyer.

Some rummagers are insistent when they are searching for special treasures. You can tell a person that you positively don't have what he is looking for, and the response will be "let me come and look anyway." Or, you can tell him precisely what you do have, and he'll come to the sale anyway. Then, the declaration is, "That's not what I want!"

Buyers' reactions are sometimes both frustrating and amusing. Sellers can spend a great deal of time creating picture-perfect, department store style displays of quality treasures, only to have rummagers stride right past them and pounce on boxes of lower quality items sitting on the floor. And, even when taller and large items are placed at the rear of display shelves, some rummagers have to push all of the short items in front of them aside, as if they're thinking, "There is something hidden there, and I'm going to find it!"

There is one aspect of sales by appointment sellers must guard against and keep under control. You must limit the available appointment times or people will take advantage of you. They'll wear you out, running you ragged working day and night. *Example:* The standard excuse for wanting to come late in the evening is, "I work all day. I can't come at any other time." But these people are often also the ones who want to come at 10:00 P.M. and browse through your treasures for two hours before spending a dollar or casually announcing, "Oh, I just came to look." Special treatment and allowances only stretch so far! These people manage to get to regular garage sales — remind them that you can be available during their lunch hour or on the weekend. If they want to get to your sale badly enough, they'll manage to.

Another problem is appointments with shoppers who fail to show up and don't bother to phone and cancel. The lack of consideration is annoying, and can cause you to lose time with serious buyers. But, this element can't be avoided or controlled. The only possible defense is to ask the customer to please call and cancel if unable to keep the appointment.

Whatever type of sale style you choose, be as creative and as different as possible!

Selling at Flea Markets

Okay — so, maybe, now you have decided you'd like to try your hand at being a flea market vendor. It's a fun thing to do, and can be profitable. *Example:* It is not unusual at all to watch one popular, well-established female flea market vendor pick up $50 in ten minutes from three customers. This particular woman has a reputation of stocking well-priced, quality merchandise, and she is always willing to bargain.

When paying for table or booth spaces at flea markets, take enough merchandise to make your investment and time worthwhile. Rummagers are there to buy! They want a good variety and a selection to choose from.

Elaborate setups are not necessary. People sell out of the back seats of cars, car trunks, and the backs of pickups. They put things in boxes on the ground or spread items on blankets. They sell off card tables, ironing boards, or make-shift tables. Anything you can set up, you can sell off. But do think about the accessibility of your setup. *Example:* One vendor displayed wares on old house doors laid on hollow concrete blocks about a foot up off the ground. Shopping was inconvenient for adults because it meant bending over, and the treasures were difficult to reach. However, as the seller soon discovered, the tables were the perfect height for curious, unsupervised children to reach breakable, sometimes valuable, merchandise.

You'll find a broad range of prices charged at flea markets. Vendors with higher prices have a smaller turnover of merchandise. Those who refuse to bargain draw smaller crowds and sell fewer items.

As a vendor, be noisy but not obnoxious. Laughter and bargaining draw crowds.

Individual flea market vendors develop reputations with regular customers. Work to achieve the reputation of being a friendly, negotiable, fair vendor who has quality merchandise with reasonable prices. Then, work to maintain that reputation if you wish to be successful. Once you have set your standards and policies, rummagers expect you to keep them. Don't make a mistake like one beginning vendor did. She quickly became known for having large quantities of interesting 50¢ items. But once her booth became established, the 50¢ items disappeared and were replaced with much more expensive objects. The vendor's business fell off. Instead of large crowds of rummagers gathering at her booth and carrying off sacks of treasures, the vendor had only occasional shoppers who browsed and went on their way without buying anything.

If you're successful at the flea market, the next stop for secondhand marketing is to open a shop. Remember, never say never! There's no telling where your passion for rummaging will take you.

Appendices

Knowledge is like money; the more he gets, the more he craves.

—Josh Billings

The wisest mind has something yet to learn.

—George Santayana

WHERE TO LOOK FOR SECONDHAND TREASURES

Secondhand treasure are everywhere! Some are right before your eyes — you may even fall over them as you walk down the sidewalk on garbage pick-up day. Other treasures may lead you on a lifelong search — they may even lead you faraway from home to distant treasure haunts.

I can't advise you on the best places to find treasures in your area; you'll need to do your own research. Ask other treasure hunters where they go; visit all the places you can think of and assess their value for yourself. Following are a few suggestions of places to start.

PLACES TO FIND TREASURES FOR FREE

Street-Picking: This is a great option if you live in an urban or suburban neighborhood. The higher-class neighborhoods make particularly prime picking for high-quality secondhand goods. Get to know the scheduled trash pickup days for heavy objects for these neighborhoods and make the rounds the night before. You'll be surprised what you might find, especially if you're willing and able to make repairs.

Junkyards: These are another good resource for finding free or low-priced goods. You may find both official, legal junkyards and not-so-official (or legal!) sites near you.

Dumps: Dump picking is a favorite pastime of many a happy rummager. Some dumps will allow you in to browse and pick; always ask before you proceed. Dumps in higher-class communities, particularly those with many summer residents, make for particularly good pickings. Some dumps or transfer stations offer an exchange site where users can drop off goods they're done with, and look for new treasures.

Classified Advertising: Newspaper classified sections often include a "For Free" section. Check this regularly; you never know when you'll hit the jackpot.

PLACES TO FIND GOOD DEALS ON SECONDHAND GOODS

Flea Markets: You can find one in almost any area of the country. City flea markets often run for several blocks.

Farmers' Markets: These weekend staples of many rural communities often include flea market items, as well as lots of delicious, fresh produce at bargain prices.

Garage Sales: Check your newspaper classifieds section for a full listing of sales on any given day.

Rummage Sales: Look for large sales sponsored by a church, a college, or a university. You can often find great bargains on everything from clothing to cast-off dormitory furniture at mark-down prices.

Thrift and Consignment Stores: Almost every urban area has a Salvation Army or Goodwill store. Become a regular at these places and you're likely to hit on some bargains.

Printed Shopping Guides: Check your local weekly free shopping guides (such as the *Pennysaver* or *Shopper's Guide*) for a full listing of individuals selling secondhand treasures.

BOOK RESOURCE LIST

BUYING

Carter, Mary R. American Junk: *How to Hunt for, Haggle over, Rescue, & Transform America's Forgotten Treasures (from Five Dollar Chairs to Five Cent Swizzle Sticks) from Flea Markets, Tag Sales, Trash Heaps, Thrift Shops, Auctions, & Attics for a One-of-a Kind Look for Your House, Apartment, Getaway, Kitchen, Bedroom — Home!* New York: Studio Books, 1994.

SELLING

Groberman, Jeff and Colin Yardley. *The Garage Sale Book: Turn Trash into Cash*. Rocklin, CA: Prima Publishing, 1986.

Gould, J. Sutherland. *Don't Throw it Out — Sell It!: Convert the Clutter in Your Closets into Cash in Your Pocket*. New York: Prentice Hall, 1993.

Hines, Jean L. *How to Have High Dollar Garage Sales: Complete Guide to an Easy, More Profitable Sale*. Choteau, OK: Vista Mark, 1989.

Hyman, Tony. *I'll Buy That Too! How to Make Easy Money Selling "Junk" Found Around Your Home & Neighborhood.* Pismo Beach, CA: Treasure Hunt Publications, 1992.

Kichler, Florrie. *Cash in On Your Garage Sales: How to Clean Out and Clean Up.* Arnold, MO: Cornerstone Press, 1992.

Kovel, Ralph M. & Terry H. Kovel. *Kovels' Guide to Selling Your Antiques and Collectibles.* New York: Crown, 1990.

Miner, Robert G. *Flea Market Handbook: Making Money in Antiques.* Radnor, PA: Chilton, 1990.

Rix, Diana. *Complete Garage Sale Kit: Everything You Need to Make Money At Your Next Garage Sale.* Naperville, IL: Sourcebooks, 1994.

Schmeltz, Les R. *The Backyard Money Machine: How to Organize and Operate a Successful Garage Sale.* Bettendorf, IA: Silver Streak, 1993.Welbaum, Bob, ed. *Garage Sale Gold.* Dayton, OH:Tomart Publications, 1992.

Williams, Michael and Pam Williams. *Garage Sale Magic! How to Maximize Your Profits — Simply and Easily!* Los Angeles, CA: Freedom Publishing, 1994.

Specific Geographical Focus

Akers, Charlene. *Never Buy Anything New: A Guide to 400 Secondhand, Thrift & Consignment Stores in the San Francisco Bay Area.* Berkeley, CA: Heydey Books, 1992.

Rovere, Vicki. *Worn Again, Hallelujah! A Guide to NYC's Thrift Shops and Other Treasure Troves.* V. Rovere, 1993.

White, Linda C. *Secondhand Shopping in Washington, D.C. and Suburban Maryland.* Washington, DC: Prudent Publications, 1993.

Repairs

Kovel, Ralph M. & Terry H. Kovel. *Kovels' Antiques and Collectibles Fix-It Source Book*. New York: Crown, 1990.

Price Guides

There are specialized price guides on everything from toothpick holders to golf clubs. If you become a collector of one particular item, you may want to look for the appropriate guide at your local bookstore. Otherwise, one of the general price guides listed below should be of assistance.

Kovel, Ralph M. and Terry H. Kovel. *Kovels' Antiques and Collectibles Price List* (26th edition). New York: Crown, 1994.

Maloney, David J. *Maloney's Antiques and Collectibles Resource Directory*, 1994-1995. Radnor, PA: Chilton, 1993.

INDEX

Page references in *italics* indicate illustrations.

A

Advertising, for garage sales,
112–14
Age of items. *See* Dating items
Alf doll, 44
Animals, stuffed. *See*
Dolls/stuffed animals
Appliances, buying secondhand,
38
Appointment selling, 127–31
At-home rummaging, 14
Automotive parts, 43
Avon bottles, 17, 33

B

Baking soda, use of, 57
Banks, 68, *96*
Bargain bags, 41, 123

Bartering, 19
Baseball cards, prices on, 15
Baskets, 48, 73, 91–92
Bathrooms, holiday decorations
in, 98
Beds, use of rollaway, 78
Beer mugs, 50, 74, 89–90
Bikes, 43
Bleach, use of household, 57, 61
Block garage sales, 10
Bonnet, lace, *35*
Books, 49
Bottles, recycling, 90–91, 93–94
Boxes, storage of items and use
of, 74, 75, 76
Brach candy tin, 36
Brasso, use of, 58
Brushes, 55, *55*

Buyers
   attracting vendors as, 118–19
   how to attract, 115–18
Buying
   appliances, 38
   asking questions, 24–26
   early bird shopping, 14
   hesitation factor, 24
   importance of comparison
      shopping, 17
   pitfalls to avoid, 23
   reasons for, 22, 23
   for resale, 108–9
   selective, 28–29
   tips for, 22–29, 108–9
   tips for buying large items, 21
   type of items bought, 4–6

C

Cabbage Patch dolls, 44–45, 50
Cabinets, recycling TV and
   stereo, 92
California Raisins, 98
Camera cases, use of, 89
Candle holders, 43, 74–76, 97
Candle rings, 44, 99, 118
Candle sconces, 82–83
Candle wax, removing, 62–63
Candy dishes, 37, 48
Casserole lids, 44
Cattle dehorner, *25*
Chamber of Commerce offices,
   10
Children, at garage sales, 115–16

Christmas decorations
   buying, 36–37, 40, 41
   cleaning, 61
   creating your own tree, 95–96
   decorating ideas using, 98–99
   decorating trees for all holi-
      days, 94–95
   as gifts, 50
   repairing, 68
   Santa Claus head mugs, 90
   tree toppers, 99
Church/charity rummage sales,
   13, 16
Cider vinegar, use of, 58–59
Cleaning
   difficult surfaces, 60–62
   solutions, 57–60
   source of information on, 54
   supplies, 53, 54, 56
Clearance sales, 28
Clothing, displaying, 121
Clown figurine, 102, *102*
Cocoa packaging, *36*
Coke glass bottles, 36
Collections, creating, 45–47
Color-coded labels
   pricing items and use of, 8, 9
   record keeping and use of, 8
   for storing items, 72
Color combinations, displaying
   items and, 85
Compass, pocket, *25*
Computers, 38
Cookie jars, storage of, 77

Cornstarch, use of, 59, 60

Costumes, 42–43

County Extension Service, 54

Curtains, made from aprons, 91

D

Dating items
color-coded labels used for, 8
magazines used for, 35
questions about, 24–25
techniques for, 34–37
UPC bars and metric measurements and, 35–36
zip codes and, 35

Declaration of Independence, 37

Decor, developing original, 80–81

Dickering and negotiating, 17–20, 122–23

Dish drainers, use of, 77, 120

Dishes
buying, 40–41, 43
dating, 37
as gifts, 48
recycling, 89–90
repairing, 69
storage of, 77–78

Displaying items
grouping of unusual pieces, 86
for selling, 119–21
shelving for, 82–84, 83
suggestions for, 85–87
windows for, 81–82

Doilies, lace, 89

Dolls/stuffed animals
Alf, 44
Cabbage Patch, 44–45, 50
clothing, 37
creating a setting for, 100, 102
decorating tips, 103–4
Raggedy Ann and Andy, 42
Smurf, 103

Drying racks, use of, 73

E

Endust, use of, 57

F

Felt items, cleaning, 60–61

Figurines
cleaning, 60
clown, 102, 102
finding, 44, 46
recycling, 96–97
repairing, 67

Fisher-Price toys, 16, 102

Flea market
pricing, 19, 132
selling, 131–33

Flowerpots
recycling, 99
selling, 116–17

G

Garage sales
advertising, 112–14

Garage sales *(continued)*

    antique prices on items, 15–16

    attracting vendors as buyers, 118–19

    block, 10

    dates and times for, 110–11

    early bird shopping, 14

    finding, 10–14

    guideposts to good, 11–14

    how to attract buyers, 115–18

    location for, 111–12

    multiple participants at, 12

    posting signs, 113, 114, *114*

    preparation for, 107–8

    preparing and displaying items, 119–21

    safety, 13

    setting prices, 121–25

    shoplifters at, 115

    walking to, 10–11

    weather conditions and, 112

    wrapping, 125–26

Gifts, secondhand items as, 47–50

Glass

    cut, 42, *85*

    painted/red, 42, 118

    ware, 50

Glass Plus, use of, 59

Gluing tips, 66

Going-out-of-business sales, 28

Grab bags, 41, 123

Greeting cards, uses for, 69

H

Hair combs, *22*

Hair spray, use of, 57

Hallways, holiday decorations for, 98

Hangers, wire, 43–44, 84

Hanging items, 73, 121

Hat peg racks, wooden, 44

Hesitation factor, 24

Home interior decorating accessories, 25

I

Inspecting items, 38–39

J

Jewelry

    boxes, 88

    collecting, 45

    displaying, 120

    for dolls, 100

    recycling, 87

    repairing, 68

Jim Beam whiskey bottles, 16–17, 91, 109, 118

Journal entries, examples of, 7

L

Ladders, bunk bed, 83

Lemon oil, use of, 57–58

Lamp, decorated stand, *11*

Library research, use of, 34

Life, 22

Liquid Gold, use of, 58

Locating items
  free items, 137–38
  good deals, 138
  tips for, 26–27, 39–41

Location(s)
  popularity trends based on, 25
  prices impacted by, 17, 33
  selling, 111–12

M

Magazines
  buying and using old, 42, 69
  dating items and use of, 35

Marble collection, 88

Matchstick holder, 33, *33*

Metric measurements, dating
    items and use of, 35–36

Miniatures, 42

Mirrors, recycling, 92

Mrs. Butterworth syrup bottle, 88

Mugs, recycling, 90

Music boxes, 68

N

Napkin holders, recycling, 91

Notebooks, three-ring, 88

P

Painting items, 63–65

Parties, suggestions for, 101

Paying, 20–21

Peanut butter, use of, 58

Peg racks, use of, 44, 73–74, 84

Photographs, use of, 9

Pictures
  hidden treasures in old, 37
  location for, 93
  restoring frames, 69

Pin cushions, 33, *33*

Plastic
  ice buckets, 89
  pails, 43
  placemats, 68
  toys, 61–62
  zippered bags, use of, 76–77

Prices
  antique prices on garage sale
    items, 15–16
  bartering, 19
  color-coded labels used for, 8,
    9, 123
  dickering and negotiating,
    17–20, 122–23
  factors affecting, 16–17
  flea market, 19, 132
  guide reference books to,
    32–33, 141
  justification for higher, 19–20
  region and location impact on,
    17, 33
  researching values and, 31–34
  setting, 8, 9, 121–25
  thrift store, 16, 19
  tips on, 14–20

Price tags, 8, 9, 123–25

Produce, seasonal, 43

Promotional items, 45

Q

Questions about items, asking, 24–26

R

Raggedy Ann and Andy dolls, 42

Recipe boxes, recycling, 91

Record albums, 45, 49, 76

Record keeping

  color-coded labels used in, 8, 9

  journal entries, examples of, 7

  photographs for, 9

  of purchase dates, 108, 109

  reasons for, 6–7

  taking notes as you rummage, 7–9

  tape recorders, use of, 7–8

Recycling items, tips for, 87–93

Relish trays, amber glass, 16

Repairing items

  basic advice, 62–70

  cracks/chips, 65, 66–67

  gluing tips, 66

  painting tips, 63–65

  supplies, 55, 56

  tools for, 53, 55

Researching values and prices, 31

  browsing and, 32

  importance of, 33

  use of library for, 34

Retail rummaging, 27–28

Rocking horse, 81, *81*

Rubbing alcohol, use of, 57

Rummagers

  definition of, vii

  importance of knowing, 26–27

  types of people who are, 3–4

Rummaging

  See also Garage sales

  church/charity rummage sales, 13, 16

  definition of, vii

  as an educational experience, 5

  as a social event, 4

  type of items bought, 4–6

S

Safety at garage sales, 13

Salt shakers, 43, 78

Scavenger, definition of, 27

Screwdrivers, 55

Seasonal decorating ideas, 94–95

Seasonal produce, use of, 43

Secondhand marketplaces

  definition of, vii

  other names for, vii

Selecting items. *See* Buying

Sellers, importance of knowing, 26–27

Selling

  advertising, 112–14

appointment, 127–31

attracting vendors as buyers, 118–19

dates and times for, 110–11

flea market, 131–33

how to attract buyers, 115–18

keeping track of purchase dates, 108, 109

location for, 111–12

posting signs, 113, 114, *114*

preparation for, 107–8

preparing and displaying items, 119–21

setting prices, 121–25

weather conditions and, 112

wrapping, 125–26

Sewing machines, 38, 88

Shelving

for displaying items, 82–84, *83*

storage and use of, 72, 73

Shirts, use of flannel, 88

Shoplifters, at garage sales, 115

Smurf dolls, 103

Soap, for cleaning, 59, 60

Socks, storage of items and use of, 74

Spice racks, 83, 93

Storage

bags (zip sealed), 77

color coded method of, 72

places for, 71–72

tips for, 73–78

Suit of armor, 39, *39*

T

Table tops/scraps, recycling wooden, 92

Tape recorders, taking notes with, 7–8

Teapots, 129, *129*

Thrift store prices, 16, 19

Tins

displaying, 86–87

for gifts, 48

storage of, 77

Tom and Jerry sets, 98

Tools for making repairs

storage of, 56

types of, 53, 55

Toothpick holders, *46*

Toys

See also Dolls/stuffed animals

buying, 16, 42, 44–45, 49

cleaning, 59, 61

creating a setting for, 100, 102

Fisher-Price, 16, 102

repairing, 70

Tree decorating ideas, 94–96

Typewriters, 38

U

UPC bars, dating items and use of, 35–36

Utility carts, 88–89

V

Values, researching, 31–34

Vases, 48–49, 60, 73

Vendors as buyers, attracting, 118–19

W

Wall groupings, 42

Wallpaper, use of, 69

Weather conditions, selling/buy-
ing and, 11, 112

Whiskey/wine bottles
    Jim Beam, 16–17, 91, 109, 118
    recycling, 90–91, 93–94

Windows, displaying items and, 81–82

Wrapping and sacking, 29–30, 116, 125–26

Y

Yarn, 44

Z

Zip codes, dating items and use of, 35